390

251

PUB

PUB

A
Celebration

Edited by

Angus McGill

LONGMANS

LONGMANS, GREEN AND CO LTD
London and Harlow
Associated companies, branches and representatives
throughout the world

SBN: 582 10121 2

This edition © Longmans, Green and Co Ltd 1969
First published 1969
Second impression 1969

Reprinted offset in Great Britain by
The Camelot Press Ltd., London and Southampton

CONTENTS

Cartoons by Blake, Eric Burgin, Gais, Graham, Hoffnung, Jak, Phil May, Pont, W. Scully, Ronald Searle, Sprod, Starke, J. W. Taylor

ACKNOWLEDGEMENTS

We are grateful to the following for permission to reproduce copyright material: the estate of the late Hilaire Belloc and Authors' Agents for an extract from 'On Inns' from *This and That and the Other*; Miss Collins, Authors' Agents and Methuen & Co. Ltd for an extract from 'A Ballad of an Anti-Puritan' from *Collected Poems* by G. K. Chesterton; Constable and Co. Ltd for an extract from *Medieval Latin Lyrics* by Helen Waddell; J. M. Dent & Sons Ltd and E. P. Dutton & Co. Inc. for an extract from *Three Men in a boat* by Jerome K. Jerome; Authors' Agents and Gerald Duckworth & Co. Ltd for an extract from *West Sussex Drinking Songs* by Hilaire Belloc; Herbert Jenkins Ltd, The Scott Meredith Literary Agency and Doubleday & Co. Inc. for an extract from *Mr Mulliner Speaking* by P. G. Wodehouse; and John Murray Ltd for an extract from *The Dear Old Village* by John Betjeman.

The illustrations are reproduced by permission of the following: pages 2, 15, 18, 21, 23, 32, 36, 38, 52, 72, 87, 149, 150, 177, 189, 210, 219, 244, *Punch*; page 60, *Evening Standard*; page 105, from Ronald Searle, *Souls in Torment* (Perpetua, 1953).

For God's sake, a pot of small ale

WILLIAM SHAKESPEARE

The Taming of the Shrew

There is something solidly, enduringly, uniquely British about the peerless British pub. Someone should congratulate us.

Other countries have their bars, saloons, beer cellars and pavement cafés and perhaps there is something to be said for them. Let someone else say it. For me it is enough that, more's the pity, none of them are pubs.

You can find pubs in foreign parts of course. In the past few years they have been cropping up in the most unlikely places. Paris, West Berlin and Brussels now have a dozen between them. There are pubs in Oslo, Nassau, the Virgin Islands. You can have a pint of peerless British beer in the Queen Victoria in Florence, the Duke of Wellington in Beirut, the Britannia in Monte Carlo, the Cock Tavern at Las Palmas, the British Grenadier in Vienna, the Lord's Pub in Garmisch-Partenkirchen. There is an extremely British pub in Tel Aviv. Prefabricated Tudor, actually.

We rejoice to see the spread of civilisation. We are proud of the onward march of British beer. But we can't help feeling for the British pub in exile, so loyal to its heritage but so very far from home.

A glass of beer in the Sir Winston Churchill in Paris is a many-splendoured thing. A mild and bitter in the Old Bell in Amsterdam is a joy for ever. But happily there is no need to go so far.

Here in Britain, where the pub began and grew to man's estate, there is a pub to welcome you round every corner.

As the old English proverb which I have just made up puts it, it's a poor street that has no pub in it. . . .

EASTER MONDAY

'Arry: 'Do you pass any pubs on the way
to Broadstairs, cabby?'
Cabby: 'Yes. Lots.'
'Arry: 'Well, DON'T!'

E. S. Turner

THE PROUD AND AWFUL ANNALS OF THE PEERLESS BRITISH PUB

I know where Men can still be found,
Anger and clamorous accord,
And virtues growing from the ground,
And fellowship of beer and board,
And song, that is a sturdy cord,
And hope, that is a hardy shrub,
And goodness, that is God's last word——
Will someone take me to a pub?

G. K. Chesterton

Chesterton's pub is one kind of pub. There are pubs where anger and clamorous accord are about as welcome as cholera. There are great family pubs with children's playgrounds. There are pubs with disc jockeys and taped advertisements. There are pubs in which one can pour confidences into the ear of a State barmaid. There are pubs which incorporate German beer cellars. There are mobile pubs and even prefabricated pubs for export.

The pub was never uniform in character, thank goodness. It has been ale-hut, tavern, victualling-house, dram-shop, inn, beerhouse, gin palace and roadhouse. There is no closer definition than the dictionary one: 'a house . . . chiefly used for selling liquor to be consumed on the premises.' To a statistician a pub is a 'drink outlet'.

The first pub was probably set up by a man who brewed better ale than his neighbours, whereupon the world beat a pathway to his door. Or the man may well have been an ale-wife. There were ale-huts, smoky hovels run by beldams, long before the Romans set up their taverns on our roads. Those taverns, like their counterparts in Rome, were meant for travellers, but folk nearby had a way of turning them into locals. In the Middle Ages ale-houses and taverns multiplied on the pilgrim routes and under their roofs one could meet all sorts of fascinating characters: minstrels, sorcerers, strumpets, pardoners, loud-roaring mercenaries, pox-doctors, coiners, gamblers, decayed troubadours, professional false witnesses, scholars and holy men willing to sell a piece of the sail from St Peter's boat. Some were content with the local ale, others called for lovely Liquid Gout from Gascony (strictly, a tavern was a wine shop). Overnight guests slept naked among the rushes. Chroniclers of those times unite to blacken the landlord's name — 'a shining example of indurated malfeasance,' says one authority. This was because Mine Host tended to be in league with local robbers, tipping them off when a prosperous guest arrived and afterwards acting as fence. Honest landlords there must have been, but who wants to know about them? The traveller was less likely to be robbed if he took his ale at the monastery guest-house, or at one of those castles which turned themselves into public-houses when the lord was away.

There were regulations for ale-houses before Parliament was thought of. Curfews curbed the noisier ones. Canterbury publicans were supposed to serve only 'such as be of good disposition and conversation'. In Henry III's time ale-conners did their best to keep up the standard of ale; bad liquor was poured down the drain or over the publican's head (he might even be ordered to drink a quantity). Otherwise, the rule was *laisser boire*. When the barons' wars ended, flooding the country with idle and licentious ex-soldiery, ale-houses became hotbeds of mischief. In 1494 a first attempt was made to limit their number and to exact sureties from those who conducted them, but by 1552 there were still 'intolerable hurts and troubles because of ale-house tippling'. In 1577 the State called on owners of taverns and ale-houses to atone by contributing towards the repair of Dover Harbour. Queen Elizabeth had her personal quarrel with publicans: the royal likeness on their signs was so vilely executed that she gave orders to burn the lot. In future only artists of approved ability were to be employed. The more eminent landlords of Elizabethan times could point to the encouragement they were giving to the drama by allowing bands of players to perform in their galleried courtyards; but not all solid citizens were convinced that the drama should be encouraged. Lesser landlords invited all who could sing, play, juggle or rope-walk to entertain — and attract — guests.

The traveller Fynes Moryson evidently felt there had been too much 'knocking' of the inn. As the Elizabethan age closed he wrote: 'The world affords not such inns as England hath, either for good and cheap entertainment after the guests' own pleasure, or for humble attendance on passengers, yea, even in very poor villages. There is no place in the world where passengers may so freely command as in the English inn.' These were welcome words; but in 1604 James I felt obliged to instruct the nation that the purpose of inns, ale-houses and victualling-houses was for 'the receipt, relief and lodging of wayfaring people', not for 'the entertainment of lewd and idle people'. The lewd and idle were unable to accept this

proposition. The hardier of them were still at it in Cromwell's time, singing deplorable songs in taverns to the
music of looted church organs. With the Restoration
came a more permissive society and the urban public-
house was once again full of fascinating characters: high-
waymen and their molls, quacks, rakes, cuckolds, jilts,
runaway apprentices, duellists and the half-pay heirs of
Falstaff. The rural pubs were more respectable. In an ale-
house on Salisbury Plain Samuel Pepys reported 'the beds
good but lousy, which made us merry'. That was just his
luck. Others had to make merry without benefit of fleas,
with nothing better than a big fire, a cosy inglenook, a
cleanly sanded floor, scrubbed deal tables, shining vessels,
fragrant hams, bowls of lavender and civil, virtuous maids
bearing good pub grub. For real civility and service,
there was the angling pub, where the landlady was always
ready to cook a man's catch, instead of groaning at the
sight of it, like a wife.

The nation was now heading for its great gin debauch.
For some time the better-off had been drinking imported
spirits. In 1690 the Government passed an Act which
allowed anyone to distil spirits, provided he gave ten
days' notice. Governments like that were rare, so the
citizens got down to gin-making while their luck was in.
Soon there was gross over-production. New dram-shops
were opened everywhere to get rid of the stuff; it was
even wheeled in barrows through the streets. The ensuing
lewdness and idleness would have broken the heart of
James I. By 1739 a survey of London by William Maitland listed 1,711 brew-houses, 207 inns, 447 taverns,
5,975 ale-houses and 8,659 spirit shops. Thus, spirit shops
accounted for more than half the city's drinking resorts.
If Maitland is right, one house in six was a public-house
and there was one public-house to forty-seven persons.

The State, which had shown more concern for revenue than for morals, tried to repair the damage with restrictive Acts. These were easily evaded, spirits being passed off as wine. How could the nation be convinced that beer was best? Some of them, as it happened, were now acquiring a taste for porter, or 'heavy wet'. Hogarth's *Beer Street* was a propagandist work. It shows plump, contented lieges drinking beer in a street where the only dilapidated building is the pawnshop (the affectionate attitudes of the couples outside the pub suggest that beer generates an unlascivious affection). In *Gin Lane* the pawnshop flourishes and all is horror.

The year 1750 is thought to have marked the high tide of Britain's carousal. After that, the authorities began to wrest some sort of control. New publicans had to produce character certificates from clergy, overseers and respectable citizens. Satirists did not neglect the Age of Gin. Ned Ward, a publican by trade, issued various coarse guides to the drinking dens of the capital. To the licensee of the Hole in the Wall at Hatton Garden he says:

> But yet take notice of a Friend's Advice,
> Folks that sell Ale should not be over-nice,
> Should not refuse in kitchen to admit
> Such customers as smoke a pipe and spit.

Which seems to show that there *were* publicans who tried to impose standards, even if they received little cooperation.

From the newspapers of the day it is clear that quacks operated freely from taverns. Vendors of pills to cure loss of memory, the side-effects of love and black damp of the soul often gave tavern addresses; though men who advertised for rich wives tended to write from coffeehouses. Professional men often used the taverns for business. But Dr Johnson put the tavern to what he deemed to be its true purpose. In a private dwelling, he told Boswell, a man was always beset by cares: 'Whereas at a tavern there is a general freedom from anxiety. You are sure you are welcome; and the more noise you make, the more trouble you give, the more good things you call for, the welcomer you are. No servants will attend you with the alacrity that waiters do, who are incited by the prospect of an immediate reward in proportion as they please. No, sir. There is nothing which has yet been contrived by man by which so much happiness is produced as by a good tavern or inn.' In short, a tavern chair was the throne of human felicity. For others, tavern life was more felicitous when the Doctor was not hogging the service.

Ownership of pubs was slowly passing into the hands of the big brewers. As early as 1726 an advertisement in the *Daily Courant* reflected the struggle in London between free and tied houses:

> A Handsome Corner Public-House, in New Belton Street, St Giles's . . . just empty, well situated and free from the Bondage of any particular Brewer.

Until roads improved, the brewers were slow to extend their influence outside the capital. But by 1818, when half the public-houses in London were tied, a Select Committee was set up to consider the system. The members acquitted the big brewers of making undue profits, but they were not wholly convinced that the poor always got the best beer in a tied house. They were told that tied houses were sometimes forced to take inferior beer from the very brewers who supplied better beer to free houses. 'Your Committee cannot reprobate in too strong terms so disgraceful a practice,' said the Report. In Chertsey the local nobility and gentry had rallied on licensing day to win the right to a free house; which was very altruistic of them, since the nobility and gentry normally depended on the beer brewed by their own butlers, even if the butlers didn't. It was, and is, the sort of controversy in which it is easier to make charges than to prove them. The brewers' case, not always heard out with true Christian tolerance, was that their backing enabled better premises to be built, more respectable publicans to be hired, and a uniformly good beer to be served to those who had acquired a taste for it; in short, they had a name to protect, and every motive to oppose adulteration, lewdness and disorder. As the nineteenth century progressed, so did the tied system; the stricter standards became, the more difficult was it for the small man to raise capital to develop a house on lines agreeable to the authorities.

It was partly with the idea of weakening the tied house system that the Duke of Wellington's Government passed that temerarious measure, the Beer Act of 1830. Its other objectives were to wean the public still further away from gin and to encourage agriculture. Henceforth any householder paying rates to the parish could open a beerhouse, without any character qualification. Overnight, the nation went back to the days before 1494. Publicans saw the Act as a malicious attack on their capital. One of them published a spirited pamphlet entitled *An Inquiry Into The Comparative Advantages The Nation Would Derive From The Appropriation of the Church Property in Preference to a Forfeiture of the Property Belonging to the Licensed Victuallers*, in which he made the point that whereas the clergy did not look after their poor and needy, the licensed victuallers did. It was soon clear that whatever was threatened, the sales of beer were not. By 1831, 30,978 new beerhouses had been opened, bringing the grand total of drinking-on-the-spot premises to 82,466. Brewers' agents toured the highways and byroads offering to pay the £2 licence on behalf of anyone interested and to extend credit; one agent from Birmingham opened 200 beerhouses in a year. The orgiastic results are suitably deplored in the 1834 Report of the Select Committee on Drunkenness, which showed that there was one drinking resort for every twenty families. The homing labourer now had to run the gauntlet, not of one beerhouse, but of four or five; and in the *louche* establishments of the back lanes, patronised by poachers and smugglers, he was not under the same pressure to behave himself as he was in the village local. In the towns the threatened publican had to fight the beerhouses as best he could — 'he gets in girls and a fiddler into the house to retrieve his ruined fortunes,' said a witness to the Select Committee. Others went all out to push the sale of gin in vastly more attractive surroundings — and the result was the 'gin palace'.

It is a mistake to suppose that the gin palace was only the old dram-shop writ large. Many an honest, old-fashioned victualling-house turned itself into a gin palace in order to fight the threat of the beerhouses. Façades were rebuilt with pilasters, caryatids and balustrades, all assembled without hint of pedantry, and the whole French-polished. These exteriors were then gas-lit with such liberality that they resembled set pieces in a firework display. When a new gin palace opened bands were hired to play in the streets and platoons of sandwichmen were sent into action. Those who were nervous about being seen to enter a gin palace found that special doors and accommodation had been provided for the use of respectable mechanics with their wives, courting couples and superior servants. Once inside, they were invisible from the street. Reformers grumbled that the only institutions which concealed their customers were public-houses and pawn shops. In fact, the multiplication of entrances to public-houses was caused in great part by that class-consciousness which more and more afflicted the nineteenth century. Foremen did not care to drink with their men, or masters with foremen. In 'servants' pubs' butlers refused to share the same floor space as footmen and footmen held themselves aloof from grooms. Hence all those saloon bars, tiny parlours, snugs, 'loose boxes' and elaborate partitions to protect the social susceptibilities of drinkers. The barman might charge the well-dressed more than he charged those with red noses and black eyes, but he was less likely to bite the half-crown offered him. The public bar remained the strident cradle of democracy: a brilliantly lit cave lined with huge barrels of Old Tom, Cream of the Valley, The Right Sort, The Dew Off Ben Nevis, Choice Compounds and (in due course) Celebrated Balmoral Mixture, as patronised by H.R.H. Prince Albert. If the customer preferred to ask for Blue Ruin or a Flash of Lightning the barman took no offence.

Then as now, many public-houses had specialist clienteles. Sporting pubs were often run by bruisers, wrestlers, jockeys, hangmen or other public entertainers; they were adorned by prints of immortal race-horses or the stuffed skins of immortal ratters. Here the Fancy rubbed shoulders with tipsters and all who hoped to profit from tipsters. Sometimes sporting landlords ran ratting pits, rats being 'obtainable on application to the barman'. Henry Mayhew interviewed Jimmy Shaw, the publican who claimed to have introduced ratting to London. He had housed 2,000 rats at a time on his premises, feeding them good barley to stop them eating each other. Advertisements in the sporting paper *Bell's Life* contained intimations like 'There will be an extraordinary number of rats destroyed on Monday evening at J. Ferriman's

Graham Arms, Graham Street, City Road' and 'dogs to destroy half their weight, in a fair wire pit'. Mayhew thought there were about seventy rat-pits in London, mostly operated by publicans. Men of fashion by no means avoided such houses. Some publicans organised live pigeon shoots, also with the assistance of *Bell's Life*; others advertised such attractions as 'a leg of mutton to be sung for by linnets', an entertainment in which caged birds were 'hung on the wall' in the public bar while a judge marked down the number of perfect notes uttered in a prearranged period of time. There was hardly any activity, from soldiering to crimping, from angling to thieving, which did not have its own public-house (you knew you were in a thieves' pub when you were asked to buy a raffle ticket to help an unlucky pickpocket). There were even mourners' pubs. One of these, on the edge of a vast London cemetery, did a marvellous trade among sob-bing, crepe-hung mourners fresh from the graveside, trying to forget that life was but a preparation for mor-tality. It enjoyed the goodwill of undertakers, who arranged to victual their horses there and suggested that the ladies might like to descend for refreshment. With luck the undertaker would buy them a drink.

The industrious publican organised any number of clubs — slate clubs, sick clubs, clothing clubs, watch clubs, clock clubs, furniture clubs, building clubs. All made for good trade. Masons met in the upstairs room and so did members of friendly societies and trade unions; but all electioneering based on public-houses was stopped in 1853. A room with newspapers was by no means rare, though some condemned this amenity on the ground that it helped to spread radical ideas. The 1834 Select Com-mittee was told of a custom whereby publicans organised gangs of coal-whippers, who unloaded the coal ships.

Only the hard drinkers, who could be relied upon to slake their thirst on the premises, were sure of a job. The custom of paying wages in public-houses, or sending a group of wage-earners with a single large note between them to the publican, to be cashed on the premises, was stopped by Parliament in 1883; and four years later the law laid down that an arrested debtor must not be taken to a public-house without his free consent or charged for any liquor unless he freely asked for it.

The sheer size and turnover of some of the pubs of Dickens' day comes as a surprise. A censorious witness told the 1834 Committee about 'enormities' which went on at the White Conduit House at Islington. This establishment had tea gardens, to which there was an admission charge of sixpence, deductible from the price of drinks. The witness, who had gone there 'from curiosity', estimated that there were between 4,000 and 5,000 visitors on Sundays, with perhaps half a dozen ordering tea. Because of riotous behaviour householders were said to be evacuating the district. Another witness claimed to have counted 269,438 persons going into fourteen London pubs in one week, including 18,391 children; an impressive feat of enumeration. Even allowing for the tendency of pub census-takers to see double, it is clear that some houses were in a very large way of business. At this time sums of £6,000 and £7,000 were often spent in rebuilding premises. As the licensing authorities began to bear down on the trade, later in the century, the value of the surviving houses often soared prodigiously. The 1897 Royal Commission on Licensing was told that the Chippenham, in Harrow Road, London, had been sold for £90,000 — 'a remarkable price for a public-house'. Its value had been artificially inflated because of a series of licensing decisions which had left it with a monopoly. A witness said that half a dozen good houses could have been operated with the same capital. Or, he might have added, a dozen or so indifferent ones, like those in the 'Devil's Acre' at Plymouth, with forty-five licensed houses in one acre, thirteen of them in one street of twenty-seven buildings.

Those who held that the finest sight in England was a gin palace in flames (and it certainly made a stirring sight, with all that liquid fuel) celebrated a big triumph in 1839, when London public-houses were forced to close from midnight on Saturday to midday on Sunday. This was a big sobering-up measure, yet still the number of beer-houses grew. In 1869 the total of licensed premises was 118,602, but by then control was once more in the hands of justices and a slow run-down of licensed premises began. The task of the bench was aided, not only by powerful temperance propaganda, but by a steady refinement of manners and a wider participation in such games and sports as did not require a public-house as base. Some justices were a prey to the belief that better amenities would only push up the rate of drinking. But if they did not know what kind of public-house they wanted, at least they were in no doubt as to the kind they did not want. They were against pubs with back doors, especially pubs which put up prominent signs directing people to the rear. Back entrances meant that bad characters could come and go, eluding the policeman keeping watch at the front. Also back doors opening on to crowded dwelling areas meant that wives and child messengers were for ever slipping in and out. The magistrates also took a harsh view of snugs, as operated in towns like Hull. A snug was a private compartment, with high partitions, dimly lighted, holding from two to half a dozen persons, with a door from the street but no access to the rest of the premises.

Sometimes the barman could see freely from his bar into the snug, but in certain premises the drink was pushed through a low aperture like that of an old-fashioned railway booking-office. Magistrates regarded snugs as inducements towards secret or illicit drinking, for example by a deceitful wife whose husband might be drinking openly like an honest man in the public bar. Justices, being men of the world, also realised that 'anything might take place' between a man and a woman in a snug. Police objected to these boxes on the grounds that the occupants were too easy a prey to thieves. It is necessary to add that snugs were often used by citizens whose only vice was a desire to avoid coarse company and by business men who regarded them as private parlours.

The justices were eager to discourage the age-old British habit of perpendicular drinking. The long bars which came in with the gin palace had been growing ever

FOGGY WEATHER

'Has Mr Smith been here?'
'Yes; he was here about an hour ago.'
'Was I with him?'

longer, with fewer tables and chairs for the consumption of 'nutritious aliments'. Stand-up bars, said the reformers, facilitated the packing in of more people; they encouraged the habit of 'drink up and go'; they discouraged sit-down conviviality yet fostered the habit of treating. Only one thing could be said in favour of stand-up bars: they were better than snugs.

There were certain reforms which the magistrates wanted to see in all public-houses: the discouragement of child messengers ferrying jugs and bottles of beer to their parents; the provision of food, thus turning the public-house back into a victualling house; and curbs on the hours of opening, especially on Sunday and in the early morning. It was easy to be sentimental about the labourer rising from a comfortless bed on a winter morning at 5 a.m. and nipping into the local, with its bright fire already lit, on his way to work; but it was a custom which, the bosses said, impaired productivity.

When public-houses were closed down, for redundancy or other reasons, financial hardship was necessarily caused. By the beginning of this century the trade had organised its own compensation scheme, based on a levy. This became effective in 1904 when Arthur (Lord) Balfour told Parliament that it would never get rid of the public-house, if that was what it was trying to do. 'I do not think you ought to get rid of it,' he said. 'What, then, should you aim at? Surely at this ideal, that the public-house should be kept respectable, should be kept by respectable persons, and should be kept in such a manner as will make those who frequent it obey the law and conform to the dictates of morality; a difficult state to attain but one which never seems to occur to a certain class of temperance reformer. Their one desire seems to be to render the tenure of the publican insecure. How can you expect the trade which you deliberately intend to make insecure to be filled by men of the character I have just endeavoured to describe?'

If there was insecurity in the air, it sometimes operated to the benefit of the customer. In the ruthless competition of those pre-1914 years there were publicans who practised 'the long pull', whereby a man received substantially more than his measure; a form of wickedness which seems to have been stamped out.

With World War I came a nasty jolt for the big brewers: the nationalised public-house. In 1916 the erection of a vast cordite factory at Gretna attracted to the area upwards of 15,000 navvies, mostly Irish, of thirsty and unruly temperament. Drunkenness convictions quadrupled and war work was held up. Under the Defence of the Realm Act the Government bought up the breweries and 321 licensed premises in the Carlisle–Gretna area. Civil servants were put in as managers, drawing no commission on sales. The policy was to stop the advertising of drink, abolish snugs, freshen up amenities, push the sales of soup and stew, prohibit the supply of drink to under-18s (not generally illegal until 1923), frown on treating and discourage the habit of chasing down spirits with beer ('a heater and a cooler'). A redundant post office was rebuilt as the Gretna Tavern. On Cromarty Firth, at the Admiralty's request, the pubs were also nationalised; and there was another take-over at Enfield Lock, Middlesex, the only area handed back to the trade after the war. The brewers resented the praise bestowed on Carlisle's model pubs by visiting sociologists and reformers; after all, they had their own improvement plans. Many of the once trend-setting premises at Carlisle now look dated; they wear the outward air of labour exchanges or dispensaries and, inside, are deficient in such delights as pictures, plaques, plush, warming pans and stuffed fish; but Home Secretaries drop in to drink a glass of Border Bitter with apparent relish.

After the war private enterprise entered on its own big improvement programme. The public-house was fighting many insidious new attractions: the cinema, the radio, the motor car (which, however, called for a new type of pub, the road-house), the rage for sport and, not least, the spread of licensed clubs (where members went on drinking after the pubs shut). There were other factors. The rehoused were under less compulsion to drink to escape their environment. The young, it was obvious, would not be content with the old-fashioned pub; nor would the

'As I always sez, Mrs Green, one 'arf the world
don't know what the other 'arf's doin'.'
'Well, that ain't your fault, dearie, is it, now?'

middle classes patronise a house with standards far below those of their own homes. Hence such refinements as the close-carpeted Saloon Lounge, with waiters to fetch the drinks, but sometimes refusing to fetch beer. In the Midlands the trade built some well-publicised show-places in the vicinity of new estates: public-houses with tea gardens, formal gardens, winter gardens, bowling greens, concert halls, children's playgrounds and much else. Of the new giants, the biggest (according to the *Guinness Book of Records*) was the Downham, erected in 1930 to serve an estate near Bromley, with two large bars holding 1,000 people, and an annexe; though the 'largest permanently available drinking space' is claimed by the Broadway Hotel at Morecambe. The new policy was sometimes described as 'Fewer and Better', or 'Fewer and Bigger', but the brewers were by no means anxious to scrap their small locals. Many citizens found the giant pubs too impersonal; Chesterton and Belloc would have hated them. The widespread Tudorising which went on is now probably regretted but architects of distinction were eventually persuaded to design pubs for the twentieth century. On the cultural front there was a cautious revival of hospitality towards strolling players, among them the Taverners who presented Shaw and Sheridan; but in Glasgow the magistrates were still fighting darts and dominoes. The pubs of the industrial back streets changed all too slowly. When the emissaries of Mass-Observation descended on 'Worktown' (Bolton) for their celebrated report *The Pub And The People* (1943) they had no difficulty in finding pubs of the earthier sort. They eavesdropped in the vault (North Country for public bar), counted caps, bowlers and trilbies, noted how often the spittoons and sawdust 'ditch' were used and with what accuracy, and recorded how long people took to sink their drinks on different days of the week. 'We have timed about a thousand drinkers. It is very laborious work,' they said. And valuable, one hopes.

The rest is familiar knowledge. Our pubs continue to change their character under social pressures. Railway inns are abandoned by their railways. Village pubs are taken over, especially at weekends, by outlying commuters. Pubs once regarded as remote appoint French chefs. East End pubs exploit the craze for 'drag'. Verse-speakers descend on drinkers at Dulwich. There are pubs which keep alive the spirit of variety; there are others where a man can still play billiards, or judge whippets. There are chi-chi West End pubs like crystal boxes. Take your pick of the 70,000-odd. Roughly, there's one pub to 750 persons, yet every person has his own pub.

Maybe there's still a mourners' pub somewhere?

One Doctor in the company who had been in England, told me that we have a Drink in England call'd Ale, which he thought was the wholsomest liquor that could go into one's Guts.

JAMES HOWELL

Epistolae Ho-Elianoe
(1737 edn.)

'. . . meanwhile, in Britain, the entire population, faced by the threat of invasion, has been flung into a state of complete panic . . .' (1940).

BONIFACE	Sir, I have now in my cellar ten tun of the best ale in Staffordshire; 'tis smooth as oil, sweet as milk, clear as amber, and strong as brandy; and will be just fourteen year old the fifth day of next March, old style.
AIMWELL	You're very exact, I find, in the age of your ale.
BONIFACE	As punctual, sir, as I am in the age of my children. I'll show you such ale! — Here, tapster, broach number 1706, as the saying is. Sir, you shall taste my Anno Domini. I have lived in Lichfield, man and boy, about eight-and-fifty years, and, I believe, have not consumed eight-and-fifty ounces of meat.
AIMWELL	At a meal, you mean, if one may guess your sense by your bulk.
BONIFACE	Not in my life, sir: I have fed purely upon ale; I have eat my ale, drank my ale, and I always sleep upon ale.

GEORGE FARQUHAR

The Beaux' Stratagem

'He only drinks to be sociable.'

✿✿

What do people drink in pubs?

Well they drink this and they drink that.

They drink whisky and vodka and vermouth and brandy and burgundy, claret, madeira and gin, port, Benedictine and lemonade shandy, rum, Bloody Mary, a small Mickey Finn, sherry, Campari, a Pernod-and-water, tomato juice, tonic and piping hot grog, apple jack, arrack, a nice glass of porter, cider and kummel and hair of the dog . . .
But the drink we drink most of, the drink we depend on, the great British tipple, the drink without peer, the drink we begin with and most of us end on is — how did you guess it? — magnificent beer.

Vincent Mulchrone

◙◙

THE GLORY THAT IS BEER

Beer is the most popular drink in the world, which downs something like 11,500,000,000 gallons of the stuff every year. Golden or black, musty or sweet, it gushes from Burton-on-Trent and Milwaukee, Dortmund, Pilsen and Munich in a flood unrivalled by any other beverage.

We in Britain account for a tenth of it. In 1967 that meant 1,131,840,000 gallons, or 20·55 gallons a head. Even so, we occupy only seventh place in the world's beer-drinking league, headed by Czechoslovakia with twenty-nine gallons a head. Then comes West Germany, Belgium, New Zealand, Australia and Austria. But we are second to none in brewing it and loving it. We have made beer part of our way of life. It is in our history, our poetry. It goes with our crops, our church, our wars, our virility.

Lesser breeds generally prefer lighter beers, and often chilled. The Englishman tends to 'chew' his beer, as if it were food. Which, of course, it is. Englishmen fanning out in search of Empire came to miss it, as they miss kippers to this day, and went to extraordinary lengths to get it. Beer has been delivered to outposts of Empire by dog sled, camel, and even balloon.

When Kipling was writing, 'You may talk of gin and beer . . .' the British Army in India sent its sick soldiers to convalesce in troopships, which sailed the Indian Ocean to get them a breath of fresh air. When they turned to hill stations, the pattern was almost invariably the same. In the first year up at, say, Mussoorie, they built a hospital. The following year they built a brewery. And there are those who say that is why Johnny Gurkha drinks his beer the same way as an Englishman, not sipping it, but getting it to the back of the throat in one throw.

The reason is very simple, though not too well known. Taste buds for sweet things are at the front of the tongue. Buds responding to bitter tastes lie further back. The idea is to drench them in one. There is no better way to quench a thirst.

Diplomats who conceive a passion for the distinctive British brew during a tour of duty in London have it shipped to some of the unlikeliest corners of earth. For some years now a 36-gallon barrel has gone each Christmas — the last part of the journey by mule-back — to one such man in Ethiopia, where beer is called *bouzah*. And it is to his part of the world — or, at least, somewhere between there and Mesopotamia — that we should raise our glass for having given us beer.

Its origin, like that of any worthwhile mystery, is decently shrouded by time. But from tombs dated 6,000 BC we have clay tablets recording the brewing of barley and water, fermented by bread. Similar tablets from Mesopotamia show two thirsty-looking characters stirring away at a brewery vat. And Babylon, we know, had the world's first barmaids. They gave good measure, too. The penalty for a short pull was death by drowning.

In Egypt, at any rate, brewing started as a priestly affair, the libation being returned to earth in gratitude for the barley that had sprouted from it. There was, presumably, a moment of time when one man had the idea of trying it himself, an inspiration ranking with the discovery of roast pork, fish and chips and the zip fastener.

Then, one imagines, came the world's first hangover. He would have to tell somebody. Hence the world's first party, the first orgy — and so on through the centuries, right down to Excise duty and keg beer.

What must have struck them very early on was that beer was far safer to drink than the water from any well or stream. The children of Israel picked up the knowledge during their bondage. It was almost certainly beer that saved them from the plague, which was probably typhoid.

But, almost from the beginning, it had its knockers. Dioscorides, a first-century Greek physician, wrote: 'Kourmi, made from barley, and often drunk instead of wine, produces headaches, is a compound of bad juices, and does harm to the muscles.' And he added: 'A similar drink may be produced from wheat, as in Western Spain and in Britain' — possibly a clue to the route beer took to these shores, for Caesar's men found us busily brewing when they landed. Sophocles, on the other hand, took a benign view. The ideal diet, he wrote, was bread, meat, vegetables and beer.

The Britons who brewed in Druidical times probably used a mixture of barley and wheat. But it was with the coming of the Saxons that ale-making got into its stride and settled the pattern of British boozing.

Tea, coffee and chocolate were, of course, unknown. Ale was the staple drink. It was not a complete beer as we now know it, because hops wouldn't be introduced until British soldiers got a taste for them in Flanders during the Hundred Years War.

Ale-feasts were the high spots of the Saxon social calendar, and it was in their day that the brewing of ale — much sweeter, heavier, and sicklier than our beer — became a treasured domestic art. One of the attributes sought in a woman was her skill as a brewster. To be able to present a fine ale at a feast was the surest way to be one up on the Saxon Joneses.

Their community life gave us 'church ales', a more roistering version of the vicarage garden party, but with the same purpose, to raise parish funds. Then there were 'clerk ales', to raise the parish clerk's stipend, and 'bride ales' from which we get the term bridal.

The Romans, a pretty fastidious lot, had given us glasses to drink from. But when they left, the British, having no time for such fol-de-rols, went back to making leather containers with rounded bottoms which fell over when set down.

Hence tumblers. Though they weren't given a chance to spill. You downed the contents in one and said 'Same again' in Saxon.

The refinement of ale was a painfully slow historical process, for there was no science to unlock the secret interaction of barley and yeast. The ale in each home or tavern was as good as its brewer, or as good as the gods which watched over the brew. The dwarfs that still decorate German beer cellars are the descendants of the wee folk who persuaded the barley to malt and the brew to come up strong and true.

It is not surprising that some of the best ale in Britain came to be brewed at the monasteries. They were usually sited by a source of good water, and the monks were able to lavish time and care on their yeast and barley.

Some of it was so good — including that from the monastery at Burton — that it was exported to the Continent. Then, as now, it was not an easy market, for the Continentals were developing their own tastes in ale. And still, as medieval travellers noted, pouring the first of the brew back on to the barley fields as a libation, just as the Egyptians had done.

In England, as the poet remembered:
Elizabeth Tudor her breakfast would make
On a pot of strong beer and a pound of beefsteak,
Ere six in the morning was tolled by the chimes
Oh, the days of Queen Bess they were merry old times.

And the Earl of Leicester wrote to Lord Burleigh: 'There was not one drop of good drink for her here. We were fain to send to London and Kenilworth and divers other places where ale was. Her own beer was so strong as there was no man able to drink it.'

It took the Hundred Years War to change the ale of old England into something like the beer we know today. Many things have been tried over the centuries in an effort to season beer before a German nun tried a plant she saw growing at the roadside — *Humulus lupulus*. The hop had arrived.

British troops liked the bitter taste it imparted. Flemish immigrants, following the boys home, saw a way to turn the liking to good account, and started growing hops in Kent. The ale brewers were not a bit amused, and petitioned Henry VI to ban the hop. Henry, to his credit — or perhaps because he had developed a taste for bitter himself — did nothing about it. But the row went on until the mid-sixteenth century, by which time the hop was king.

One of the best known varieties of hops in this country bears the charming name 'Fuggles', after the hop grower who spotted it as a 'sport', a chance variation in the character of the plant.

By the way, only the cone-like fruits of the female hop plant are used. The males play havoc with a brew — though even the female hops plays no part in the brewing process. They are introduced at a late stage for their flavour and their slight preservative effect.

But the basic principles have changed little in thousands of years. It is just that the secret art has become a science.

The main raw material is still barley, which is malted, that is, made to sprout by heat. The barley has in it insoluble starch, together with enzymes which are necessary to make the starch soluble in water. The grain is allowed to germinate under carefully controlled conditions, then heated to stop the growth. This is the maltster's art. The malt is then crushed and mixed with hot water, which allows the enzymes to change the starch into sugarlike substances. The liquid, or wort, is then drawn off.

The hops are added at this stage and the liquid boiled again to stabilise and sterilise it, and to extract the flavour from the hops. The enzymes are destroyed in the boiling.

Yeast goes into the cooled wort to ferment the sugars and produce alcohol and carbon dioxide. Your average pint today is the product of about a quarter of a pint of barley malt and six hops. The primary fermentation takes about a week. The yeast is then drawn off and the beer — though you would turn your nose up at it at this stage — is ready for conditioning. How long it is then kept, and its treatment, varies according to whether it will finally emerge as draught, bottled, kegged or canned.

The brewers guard their yeast jealously, keeping it in spotless, white-tiled cells. It was whilst he was looking for a way to safeguard brewer's yeast that Louis Pasteur hit upon his theory of pasteurisation. For it was he who, in 1876, discovered that yeast was responsible for fermentation. Under less scientific conditions than those of today 'wild' yeast in the air had been polluting the brewer's yeast and causing poor fermentation.

The chemical break-down of a good pint of beer goes something like this: water, 90 per cent, alcohol, 4·5 per

cent; carbohydrates, 4·3 per cent; protein, 0·4 per cent;
salts, 0·3 per cent; vitamins, colouring, flavouring, 0·1
per cent. Its colour, contrary to pretty wide belief, is no
indication of strength. The darker colours of some beers
are simply due to roasting the grain. The alcohol content
in strong beers can go as high as 10 per cent of alcohol,
the strength of a light table wine, and there are drinkers
who wish that more of it was made.

The difficulty goes back to the reign of Charles II,
when the government fixed a form of taxation which still
exists — the stronger the beer, the higher the tax. But
taxation increases. And the average beer drinker's pocket
is not bottomless. So the brewers have little option but to
reduce the strength of the beer. It is a pity, because the
names of some of the stronger beers ring like a challenge
— Winter Warmer, Brewer's Pride, Poacher Ale, No. 1
Extra Special, and Stingo. The latter, incidentally, was in
use in the eighteenth century, when other beers had
quaint names like Huff-cap and Nipitato.

The strength of a man's beer, relative to that drunk
elsewhere in the country, is a constant source of local
pride and inter-regional argument, especially the eternal
North v. South wrangle. And it will probably continue so
to the end of time. For the simple fact is that there are
close to 3,000 different brands of beer in Britain today. If
you drank a different beer every day in an effort to settle
the argument, it would take you eight years to get through
them all. Only, by then, you probably wouldn't care.

All the same, it is probably true to say that the beer gets
fractionally stronger the further north you go, with
pockets of extra strength in the great industrial conurba-
tions where men doing heavy work have always de-
manded 'beer you can bite'. Steel cities like Sheffield,
shipbuilding cities like Newcastle and Middlesbrough,

have always taken pride in their strong brews, which they see as being complementary to their masculinity. In such places, as indeed throughout the country, it is a high compliment to say that a man is a good judge of a pint. Yes, but what sort of a pint. What beer? What strength?

Quite apart from the reduced strength of beer forced on us by taxation, public taste has changed — indeed is constantly changing — and the beer-drinking pattern is very different from what it was at the turn of the century. Then, there were 102,000 'on' licences in this country. Now there are about 69,000. Then there were only 6,500 licensed clubs. Now there are 24,000. In 1914 there were over 1,000 brewery firms. Now there are 110.

Now there are women in the local, looking for a lighter beer, a sparkling beer, one that looks pretty in a glass. Our social habits have changed, the pubs have changed with them, and the beer is changing with both. Before the last war, 60 per cent of the beer we drank was mild. By 1963 the pattern had changed to 33 per cent mild; 25 per cent bitter; and 36 per cent bottled and canned.

The other 6 per cent showed the first real impact of keg beer, an innovation still arousing strong passions in pubs around the country. Keg beer comes in metal canisters, and is sped on its way to the glass by carbon dioxide. It signalled the end of the traditional wooden barrel, and coopers, one of the oldest crafts, started turning barrels into garden furniture. It made the bar pump redundant, and the very look of the local changed when all the landlord need do was turn on a tap. Its advantages were immediately obvious. The carbon dioxide not only pumped the beer to the glass, but the gas remaining in the canister helped preserve the beer so that there was little or no chance of it going off.

At last a beer which no landlord could spoil. And a boon to those establishments with only an intermittent trade — a Rugby club bar, for example — for the keg beer would keep much longer.

As the brewers put it, 'A beer which is a distinct "quality" product, with a consistent character and high visual appeal'. But the equipment was costly, and the canister beer cost from 2d. to 6d. a pint more than the best bitter, depending on the bar.

A howl of protest went up from the traditionalists, some of whom formed The Society for the Preservation of Beers from the Wood. Members wear black (for mourning) ties decorated with (wooden) barrels. It is a condition of membership that a man will not drink keg beer unless a pint from the wood is not available within a radius of half-a-mile (if on foot), or of five miles if in a car.

And the society published a lament:

> Keg, or not to keg; that is the question.
> Whether 'tis nobler for the gut to suffer
> The effect of CO_2 in dustbin beer
> Or take arms against the sea of bubbles
> And, by boycott, to end them . .

The anti-keg brigade claim some victories, as when a small brewery in the South took over a 'keg' pub, pulled out the detested modern equipment, and went back to wooden barrels and the beer that used to be. But by and large 'keg', with its appeal to women and to young people, seems to be winning. As 'keg' landlord say, 'How can anybody tell the difference? The barrels were coated inside, and so are the canisters.'

However, the extra carbonisation, and even the very fact that 'keg' has a consistent character, is sufficient to keep going the sort of controversy that is the breath of life to a pub.

It has always been part of a 'real' beer drinker's ritual to deride his fellow's choice of drink. Bitter looks down on mild. Both tend to sneer at bottled beers, though there was a giant swing to bottled beer during the 1950s. And there was a time, not long ago, when all three joined forces to deride lager as an insipid Continental substitute for real beer which would never take on here. They have been proved wrong.

Lager sales have almost doubled in the past four years. And, with the exception of the very old, it has gained ground with every kind of beer drinker, not only with the sophisticated young. As beers go, it is still a youngster, born in Germany little more than 120 years ago. Its name simply means 'storage'. What was revolutionary about it was that it turned the fermentation procedure upside down. The yeast started from the bottom instead of the top, took more than twice as long to do the job at much lower temperatures — but produced a distinctive, and occasionally distinguished, brew.

It, and many non-lager beers of its type, should be served cold. But here we hit another of the great beer controversies — not regional, but by now international.

The American says the Englishman prefers his beer tepid. This is not the case. What the American calls tepid, in relation to beer, is what the Englishman calls cool. In witness of that, there are pubs in Britain, their cellars cut in dripping limestone, which have been magnets to connoisseurs of a cool, well-kept pint for centuries.

In a blazing New Zealand summer it is the habit to drink beer from glasses no bigger than a sherry schooner, the theory being that such an amount of beer will not have time to change from its near-frozen state before it is drunk.

And the incredible lengths some people will go to to get cold beer command a certain awe, if not necessarily respect. One effort which commands both concerns a squadron of American Navy dive bombers whose pilots found themselves sitting on a very hot Pacific island facing some very warm cans of beer. Whenever the need became urgent, they loaded a number of cans into the ammunition storage bays in their wings, climbed to the coldest air they could find, and then streaked back to base before the tropical heat had time to affect the precious cargo.

A long haul from the Nile valley, where it may have begun, to 20,000 feet above the Pacific Ocean. But then, the liquid staff of life has played many parts through the ages. Few drinks have attracted such fancies, so many myths, such appealing loyalties. In one breath it is the most fascinating subject, and in the next the most infuriating.

People drink it, in some of its forms at any rate, to put on weight. Yet it is not fattening. A pint of light beer has no more calories than five ounces of lean meat, or a pat of butter.

It is the little man's drink because it is held to be cheap. Yet if you look at the amount of alcohol you are getting it is one of the dearest drinks in the world.

It is as foreign as tea in origin yet, like tea, the British have made it somehow their own. As the Rev. Sydney Smith said early in the nineteenth century, 'What two ideas are more inseparable than Britannia and beer?'

The brewing industry — or 'The Beerage' as its moguls have been unkindly called — are fond of pointing out that it is 'the beverage of moderation'. And so, nowadays, it is.

But there lingers in the British consciousness the knowledge that it was not always so. Sir John Barleycorn once ranked with Saint George in the Englishman's imagination.

There are sober historians to this day who say it is a wonder that Englishmen got through the Middle Ages without falling flat on their national face and letting in the French with their wine, and suchlike nonsense. But we never lost our passion for ale. Though the distinction, and the word, has become meaningless, 'ale' is still used as a manly, vigorous way of saying beer. If a man can 'hold his ale', there can be little wrong with him. Go into a country pub at mid-day and hear a group of friends tell each other, 'We shifted some ale last night. Hey, didn't we shift some ale last night?' It is not a bad boast, for it claims no more than companionship and good cheer in a manner that is as old as England herself.

For the story of beer is woven inextricably into our history. Saxons drank the health of their newborn in it.

Elizabethan housewives cooked with it. Though we seem to have neglected the art, it does well for casseroles, batters, ham and rabbit — and just a drop adds bite to a Welsh rarebit.

Beer was for bride-feasts. Beer, in yards of ale, was for fun. Some literally took it with them to the grave.

> Poor John Stott lies buried here
> Though once he was both hale and stout,
> Death laid him on his bitter bier.
> In another world he hops about.

There have been grander epitaphs. But few that could so mirror the light in the eye of an Englishman as he raises his ale to his lips and wishes the world 'Good health'.

'It SHOULD be all right, Ted — I've just put on a new barrel.'

'Very well,' said Mr Pickwick, 'then we will stop here.'

'Lights in the Sun, John; make up the fire; the gentlemen are wet!' cried the landlord. 'This way, gentlemen; don't trouble yourselves about the post boy now, sir. I'll send, him to you when you ring for him, sir. Now, John, the candles.'

The candles were brought, the fire stirred up, and a fresh log of wood thrown on. In ten minutes' time, a waiter was laying the cloth for dinner, the curtains were drawn, the fire was blazing brightly, and everything looked (as everything always does, in all decent English inns) as if the travellers had been expected, and their comforts prepared, for days beforehand.

CHARLES DICKENS

The Pickwick Papers

Pubs have always attracted great talkers. They still do. The man who complained that the art of conversation was dead must have been a teetotaller . . .

'Oh, no, not another repeat night on the telly!'

Basil Boothroyd

FEAST OF REASON, FLOW OF SOUL

I suppose I've been unlucky, if you care to put it like that, but I've never yet struck one of those pubs where strolling players are standing the saloon bar a poetry recital. I believe there's a lot of it about, but it's hard to say just what sort of experience it is, whether for the management, the performer or the saloon bar.

The landlord, I take it, gets some advance notice of what's going to hit him. It must be a nasty shock, otherwise, when this youth with the sensitive-looking Adam's apple uncoils himself from the inglenook — where he's been an hour over a small bitter, getting his nerve up — and suddenly yells out,

> I Tiresias, though blind,
> Throbbing between two lives,
> Old man with wrinkled female breasts ——

'Now, now,' says the landlord, pumping a lot of beer on to his boots. '*If* you please. What's going on here, do you mind?'

'T. S. Eliot,' says the youth.

'I don't care who you are. Kindly watch your language, that's all. This is a clean house we keep here, all right?'

Bad luck, lad, you should have set things up first. You'll learn in time that nothing in life comes off without a bit of prepared groundwork, from summit meetings to improper suggestions. Once you've made your number with the licensee, and he's agreed to hammer on the bar with a tankard, and announce to his clientele that they're in for the collected poems of Louis Macneice, with mandolin and bongos, they'll hitch their chairs round and prepare to take it. Well, you might get a couple of dissenting voices, one of them indignantly four-lettered who says all he wanted was a quiet ——ing pint, and if he's got to have the Third ——ing Programme thrown in he'll take his custom to the Half ——ing Moon; the other, a feebler spirit, says he'll just pop out and see if his car lights are on, and doesn't come back.

And the second one could easily be me, I'm sorry to say. This shows me up in a rotten light. Your born pub-goer, or Natural Frequenter, goes along with the philosopher Terence: he is a man, and nothing human is alien to him. I don't say that he lines up for opening time with these actual words on his lips, but the sentiment's there: a foot across the threshold and he's a citizen of no mean city, safely within the gates. Outside, the boss, the income-tax man, the wife; inside, his accepted fellow creatures; just being in there is the only qualification he asks for, whether they're wandering minstrels — and in your cavernous London pub with a hundred-foot bar, slopped all its length, even amateur pop groups are tolerated, even applauded, as they rend the distant, smoke-filled shadows with their specially distorting microphones — or just crushed, muttering old men with string belts and a secret grievance. For all he cares, as a matter of fact, they could be bosses, income-tax men, or even wives: and that's fine too, as long as they're not his. The pub bathes the lot of them in its benevolent golden light, and I don't mean the stuff generated by the Electricity Board. This light is of the soul.

Come to think of it, I never heard of anyone having a drink in a pub with his income-tax man, or anywhere else, for that matter. Encounters traditionally take place in a green steel office. Men have been known to drink with their bosses, it's true, but this is a travesty of public-house practice and procedure, where the essential level-ling properties of the pub are frustrated from the start. A keen observer can spot the unnatural association a mile off. Its hierarchical distinctions cry aloud. No boss would laugh with that note of ready hysteria, keep trying to buy two rounds running, not only distribute cigarettes but light them, or be the first to drink up and leave; no under-ling would hook his umbrella on the bar just where it's convenient for the other chap to put his glass, or dismiss a humorous angling story with a nod and say, 'What hap-pened, by the way, about Amalgamated Trawlers and the fish-glue claim?' Oh, no. The master and man relation-ship is for business, or unlicensed, premises. The pub is not for soiling. Even the introduction of wives is not in the true liberal spirit of the place. There are inhibitions. The husband's usual rapport with the barmaid is muted on these occasions; he tends to be formal and stiff when the resident wit comes weaving over with his latest variant on the bishop and the actress: bringing himself to say things like 'a small port' is a drain on his nervous system that reverses the balmful properties of the whole exercise, and when she says, 'That's your lot, George, you'll be up all night', and snaps her handbag shut, he can feel the bar's winks and nods on the back of his neck all the way to the door.

This isn't to say that there aren't certain happy couples who are more at home in the pub than they are at home. You might wonder if they've got a home, considering they're always in the pub. There they are in the same old corner, well past the hot-blooded years, but still exchang-ing the occasional melting glance between their refined sips of draught stout. Got up for the ceremony, too, with a froth of crisp, ruched blouse, best stockings and Mum's cameo brooch on the one side, and smart boots, stiff sports jacket (sometimes with matching cap) on the other. And a pretty and touching sight they make.

Any marriage counsellor who happens to drop in should feel well pleased with himself. Hasn't he spent all day advising dissident couples to find a common interest? The thing's paying off before his very eyes. It might have been bowls, archery, Old Tyme dancing, or a shared obsession with glued-matchstick cathedrals: as it is, it's this harmonious boozing, and always with decorum. We've been together now for forty years, and never a drop too much. Possibly a touch of the Nellie Deans on a Saturday night, a traditional time for singing, but that's about all.

Your regular had his doubts at first about this enclave of married bliss. Was this what pubs were for? Wasn't it, on the contrary, just what they weren't for? But he soon accepted them, not least because of their proper respect for the place and the occasion. Anyone who dresses for Royalty when the nearest they're going to get is the Queen's Head is all right by him. He has strict views on this sort of ceremonial. Slipping round to the pub in your old television trousers and yesterday's shave is no way to treat the place.

He himself, as a matter of fact, tends to hoard up his shave until the evening, when the drinking hour strikes, and a clean shirt to go with it. He doesn't owe the office, shop or assembly line anything in the way of sartorial tribute. Stuff the office. Who's going to notice, anyway, if he hasn't trimmed out his ear whiskers and checked his socks for tautness? The pub's different. It's the proper respect you want, not only giving but receiving.

PUB

Fred the landlord, who's once more transformed the place from last night's reek of piled ashtrays and trampled potato chips into a swept, aired and ordered palace of delight, the stack of charity pennies aligned on the bar, the horse brasses winking in the glow from the electric log-fire, deserves no less: not only in his own right as Mine Host (whose portrait, with a big head and tapering body, is framed behind him with the caption 'Mine Host'), but as the anointed representative of that greater power, the entire licensed victualling trade. Of pubs, that is. In my father's house are many mansions: this is the one you've picked, and you're going to do it proud.

Not only that, let's be honest, but there's your own standing to think of. What's Fred going to get, as the door, sticking a little, bursts open out of the night? None of your battered hats and disordered moustaches, but you, smart as a whip and raring to go, tie-clip dead centre, complexion buffed to a high gloss, nails fit to pass a kitchen staff inspection at Claridges, and palate expectantly tingling from a discreetly mint-flavoured dentifrice.

Have you seen but a bright lily grow, Before rude hands have touch'd it? Have you mark'd but the fall of the snow, Before the soil hath smutch'd it? If not, now's your chance. It all has the crisp, pre-gladiatorial air of a clean, scrubbed, printless pitch at Lord's before the first ball is bowled, or the pure green swathes of Wembley — and what about saying a kind word for the British licensing laws in this connection? It hadn't struck you, perhaps, that without them the great twice-daily national ceremony of Opening Time would be lost to us: no sense of occasion, no zest of anticipation, thrill of delayed delights. You may be able to get a drink whenever you fancy one in those stained old crummy round-the-clock Continental bistros; only here, in the land of the unfree,

43

can we savour the springlike sensation, twice a day, of
life beginning anew.

Oh, yes, the scene may suffer a bit as time goes by, the
arena become scarred, worn and generally disarranged,
they may even have to bring the sawdust on; but let's
start right, shall we? When Fred looks up from buffing a
sparkling glass with a snow-white cloth and says, as he
always says, 'Well, Charlie?' and you say (as you always
say), 'Well, Fred?' let nothing mar the sweet rapport of
these exchanges. The formalities over, you can move on
to wider fields, the conversation blowing where it listeth.
A sticking door is as good an opening as another.

'Door still sticking, then, Fred.'

'What door's that, then, Charlie?'

'Your door. Sticking again.'

'Ah. When they painted it.'

'Ah. Been a lot of rain, too. Going to take a little
something, then, Fred?'

'Bit early for me, Squire, thanks all the same.'

'Cheers, then.'

'All the best,' says Fred, raising an empty hand a few
inches off the bar in a token toast. 'It was George Finney's
boy,' he says.

'Do what?'

'Painting. Started this bit of a painting firm down the
housing estate, with young Wassname.'

'Jack Wills?'

'Used to be a postman.'

'Young Billy Shipley?'

'I shall be forgetting my own name next,' says Fred.
'Sister married one of the Friths.'

'Bert Frith? Short, glasses, worked on the railway?'

'No, I tell a lie. Not Frith. Lanky, with a — excuse me a
tick. Well, Arthur?'

PUB

Its difficult for landlords. No favouritism. Even when you've got the cut and thrust of debate going full belt like this, you can't let your next regular go ungreeted. The skilled licensee, besides knowing about beer, needs the social techniques of a Mayfair dinner hostess, and bringing a newcomer into the cosy circle without leaving the old one out in the cold is a neat trick. It doesn't matter so much with strangers. Your passing car-trade, especially if it leaves its consciously impressive car ostentatiously visible outside the window, can be left to cool its self-importance until priorities are satisfied, or until it puts its foot right in it with some such ill-judged remark as, 'Landlord, what about a little service here, if you'd be so kind?' (This, in fact, only adds another five minutes to the delay; and five minutes is a long time when every staunchly loyal eye in the bar is turned on the misguided foreigner, their converging laser beams burning into his aplomb until he fancies he can smell it burning.) Regulars, it's different. Your true landlord sees in a flash how to hook up the independent elements, thus keeping every-one mellow and swelling the flow of soul. He need only say, as he delicately draws Arthur's usual, that he's been telling Charlie about young Finney's decorating business...

'Cheers. First today,' says Arthur. 'Down the housing estate, you mean. Teamed up with young Wills.'

'Told you it was Jack Wills,' says Charlie, moving to a nearer stool. 'Fred's door's sticking,' he says.

And from there the talk can take fresh wing in limitless directions. Paint quality today . . . and you're into tele-vision commercials . . . in no time you're through David Frost, pop music, a televised Parliament, framehold trouble, do you take your aerial out in a thunderstorm and last night's documentary on Famous Nuns of Tibet: it could stop there, because you don't want to get on to religion, but it doesn't matter, because somebody else has come in now, picking up the thunderstorm bit with a story about a golfing friend who won't have a zip-fly because he's afraid of being struck by lightning . . . that way lie the anecdotes, clean and dirty, and that ancient, mystifying probe about where they all come from . . . you're not going to tell *me* that stockbrokers are capable of — mind you, they say they're the same ones, keep coming round . . . of course, in the days when commercial travellers *were* commercial travellers . . . by the way, did you hear about poor old Percy Wainwright? Oh, yes, must be a month ago now, his wife took his mug of tea down to the greenhouse, Sunday morning, and there was poor old Percy . . . And that one can branch out all ways: life insurance, car insurance, cars, prefab garages, Do-it-Yourself, even back to paint, Fred's sticking door, 'Ah, well, it's the damp, look at the rain we've had . . .' and once you're on the weather you're home and, as you might say, dry.

Nothing, you'll notice, Johnsonian. Any Boswell in your true, acceptable pub, poised to snap up the gems, the aphorisms and profundities, would be still sitting with an empty notebook at the Time Gentlemen Please. Sam Johnson, I imagine, emptied any pub he was ever in by the time he'd got out his first, 'Sir — !' Good talk has its place, I daresay. Let it go to it and stay there. It isn't the quality of the talk, but the fact of it, that makes a pub. A few generalities about politicians may be all right. Just rough judgments: power-crazed incompetents, shoot the lot, that sort of thing — with mine host watching warily between the beer handles to see the place isn't deteriorating into some sort of Parliament or similar rough house: you can never be sure some more specifically opinionated spirit hasn't been lurking behind his pint, ready to erupt with his personal solution for the troubles of the nation, the world, and the moon, very likely, if the talk isn't damped down into more interesting and agreeable channels, such as how many days you can shave with one blade, or the best way to get from Coventry to High Wycombe without being caught ten miles from a pub at opening time.

No, no, the world outside, at present scared off by the lights and the laughter, is only too ready to pounce once we rejoin it, with its claws at the ready. Wars, famine, pestilence; the tax man, the trade gap, the ills of the flesh, the wife's relations. They can be touched on in the pub, bravely derided, but they're not real in there, they can't get at you. In any case, they aren't the proper study of the pub-going man: any evening paper lying around on the pub tables is folded with the sports page showing. Nobby Stiles, racing at Kempton Park, fine. The headlines about economic chaos or tanks on the move in the Carpathians are rightly tucked under.

What's to be said, anyway?

There's an enduring fiction about the man in the pub: it concerns his rough, native wisdom, that earthy, untutored British commonsense that pierces right to the nub and core of problems that have had the United Nations by the ears all its life. The truth about the man in the pub is that he never says anything worth saying, and quite right too. Let others, in other places, shout down the student cat-calls and dodge the thrown fruit. The man in the pub feels just as purged and stimulated after a feast of reason that gets no deeper into the destiny of man than the Council's new one-way street plans, or a good place to get tyres at 30 per cent off, as if he'd been making a major speech on nuclear non-proliferation before a crowded House. Probably more so.

There are pubs, of course, though barely worthy of the name, where such delights of intercourse can never hope to get off the ground. These reflections, in the main, have concerned the ideal pub (and the strange thing about the ideal pub is that, unlike most ideal concepts it actually exists. We all have one. Strange but true.) But there are others.

There is the pub, for instance, misguidedly got up as the inside of a galleon, a Western saloon, or, for all I know, St George's Chapel, Windsor, or a Jumbo Jet. For my money — and I suppose that's what they're after, in their hopeless, twisted way — they can send all this stage-property rubbish back to the scene store at Riverside Studios. Who's going to get a decent conversation going with a Ye Olde Shippe's Plastick Lanthorn burning its sixty-watt bulb in his ear, or a lad swabbing the tables dressed as something out of a Dodge City gunfight? There's a rule on these joints, incidentally: the fancier the fittings, the worse the beer. Perhaps even the beer feels sour about it.

Or there's the pub where you can see at a glance that the couple in charge are too good for the licensing trade, and know it . . . Such fun, darling, haven't you heard? — Torquil and Philippa, taken a pub, darling — but of *course* they don't know a thing about it, never mind, all the old crowd are going to run down there at weekends, you won't *see* the place for Jags, darling . . . All right, mid-week only for me, then, if at all, might just be a chance to fight my way to the bar through the management's screaming old pals . . . Even so, landlords in crested blazers and club chokers tend to put me on some sort of social mettle I haven't got, which impairs true, natural enjoyment; and their lady wives don't help when they're called in from their day-bed to find the angostura: they tend to appear with marked petulance, in jodhpurs, accompanied by an immense well-bred dog and complaining that they were just going to ring up Mummy. Can't find the angostura, either, and if you don't watch it you can get Worcester sauce in your gin.

No, I've nothing against people taking a pub for their own amusement. All I ask is that they don't throw it open to the public.

There are pubs where the canned music is loud, continuous and apparently unnoticed, so that when you shout a request for it to be taken down a notch they don't know what you're talking about. There are pubs whose tables are uniformly designed with one short leg, and when the man opposite lifts his beer off, yours dips an inch, and your knees are awash; pubs with barmaids who only took the job because of the chance it gives them to get off smart cracks . . . or landlords who keep saying, 'Be with you in a minute' from the other bar, and go on with a leisurely stacking of innumerable crates until your thirst is well past its prime; there are pubs run by arrogant lone women, who entice the hungry traveller with eye-catching billboards about freshly-cut sandwiches, and when he's pulled off the road, parked, locked the car and walked back, receive the word sandwich as if it's a new addition to the language: there's some inscrutable private rule, it seems — no sandwiches after two, or before eight, or on alternate Tuesdays.

There is no ease in such places. You are there on sufferance. Have your right money ready, drink up and get out, and if you're one of those ingratiating softies who helpfully return their used glass to the counter, don't look for thanks.

But the negation of all pubs is the pub that's for nothing but drinking. This is a pub of the towns, usually hiding

its shame in the mean back streets, and stumbled on
only by black accident. The lights are low, the floors wet,
the faces lining the wall disconsolate. No word is uttered.
The elbows rise and fall under a leaden compulsion. The
smoke-smeared decor is olive green, the only relief a
curling pin-up from a tradesman's calendar of three years
back, to which someone, in an inconceivable excess of
high spirits, has added Laughing Cavalier whiskers. It's
the only laughter there. Mine Host is a mere human beer-
engine, the pot-boy a septuagenarian wreck. A line from
Captain Scott's diary springs irresistibly to mind: 'My
God, this is an Awful Place!'

I said at the beginning that I wasn't a Natural Frequenter, and it's this sort of pub, I think, that could
account for it: not directly, but by a proxy trauma of my
early years. I was brought up on the creed that drink was
the root of all evil, and the Public House (my parents gave
it audible capital letters, as they would Hell and Beelze-
bub) its compost heap. We lived in the colliery area of Not-
tinghamshire, where the streets filled after closing time
with unsteady miners, behaving peculiarly even to a child-
ish eye. 'Take no notice,' my parents would say, strategi-
cally crossing the road or hiding my eyes in a handy
doorway. 'Poor fellow, he has been in a Public House.'
Poor fellow, indeed. His pub, I fancy, must have been one
of the Awful Places. When I left home I promised,
and eagerly, never to pass through the Door of Shame.

Ah, well. Promises. I soon fell. It was a turn of fate,
perhaps, that my first branch of the bank was in a town
with more pubs per head of the population than anywhere else in the country. It was hard to miss them. I
remember keenly my deep sense of sin as I allowed myself
to be led into one of them by a wicked ledger-clerk friend.
What nameless orgies lay in store?

PUB

It was a shock, finding the place clean, bright and empty, but for the motherly creature behind the bar and — could it possibly be? it was — the Vicar. The firelight glittered on the brasses and glasses. The Vicar saw his poster for the Old Folks' Tea duly pinned up, and departed. The landlord appeared, scrubbed, starched and courtly. The regulars began to trickle in, some of them, to my amazement, respected customers of the bank.

'Well, Fred?'

'Well, Charlie?'

I'd seen worse orgies at Missionary Exhibitions, to which I'd been considerably exposed, and my first impulse was to write home and tell them what they'd been missing all this time. I suppressed it. You can't budge fixed thinking.

But it's made me, as you'll gather, a bit selective all my life. And aware, as some people are not (including temperance organisations), that when it comes to pub-going, the booze is the least part. What matters is the flow of soul.

'CANCELLED!!... the darts match?'

❁❁

*There are moments in a pub when all talk, however good, dies
away. There's a breathless hush in the bar tonight, the game's at
stake and the champion's in. One carefully judged dart and it's the
Hallelujah Chorus and drinks all round. Meanwhile even the
dominoes hold their breath.*

*Pubs have nurtured many games, games worth the attention of a
serious-minded man, games demanding a contemplative nature, a
keen eye, a steady hand and a frequently replenished pint of best
bitter. These are, say some, the best games. These are, say others,
the only games . . .*

Anthony Hern

A VERY NICE DART

This friend of mine, an otherwise intelligent person of manly frame and cheerful countenance, suddenly decided to take the game of shove ha'penny seriously. He had somehow reached the brink of middle-age and fought through a whole war without ever applying skill and touch to the art of sending a smooth coin-like disc gliding over a polished board. When I introduced him to the game he made the usual miserable start — for, like many a village pastime, there is a great deal more to shoving half-pence about than meets the supercilious eye. But his game improved slowly. Too slowly for him. Perhaps he got tired of being always beaten by more experienced players, thus having to fork out for the opposition's regulation half-pint at the end of every game. I cannot think that there was a purse-pinching motive behind what he now did, though it is true that the most generous stander-of-rounds is liable to weaken at the sheer monotony of the hand-pocket-barman-cheers routine if it seems likely to be prolonged to infinity. I think that what happened was that he became peeved at the thought that men of lesser calibre than he, smaller men, even ill-favoured men — men such as I, in short — could give him a licking any time between 7 p.m. and 8 p.m. on weekdays, half an hour later at the weekends, at the table in the south-east corner of the saloon bar of the Station Hotel. What he did was to buy, in what I take to be slightly shamefaced

secrecy, a shove ha'penny board of his own and practise
privately in his own dining-room. Later, his wife was
brought to admit that he played quite well at home.
Indeed, so eager was he to startle both opponents and
kibitzers in that same south-east corner, that he gave up
his evening visit to the saloon bar in order to bring his
game to championship pitch, much as Arnold Palmer
might give up smiling in order to make sure of winning
another hundred thousand dollars in a golf masters'
tournament. The day dawned — or, to be strictly accur-
ate, the sun set — when he returned purposefully to his
old haunt to silence the scoffers and start on a lifetime of
well-earned, free half-pints of Mann's I.P.A.

It was not to be.

The skill he had so laboriously acquired on his shop-
bought board deserted him as soon as he crouched over
the slightly pock-marked, ill-lit, dearly-loved board that
is the Station Hotel's most cherished possession. He was
the same old fair-to-middling player with whom we had
become familiar. As he paid up yet again at the end of that
first game, his language, like his countenance, tended to
the florid.

But he had learnt one important lesson the hard way.
It is this: pub games belong in pubs.

As the shamrock to Ireland, or the puffin to Lundy
Island, so there are certain games that wither and die away
from the atmosphere of a pub. Indeed, as we shall see,
there are some games that are *never* played anywhere but
in a pub. And even games that you'd think would be
harmless, even pleasurable, outside a pub tend to become
pale imitations of the real thing, like near beer. Let anyone
who is at this moment thinking of enlivening his happy
home by installing a dartboard in that alcove by the
living-room table think again. There's nothing wrong

with a dartboard as a piece of decor if you can't afford a Kandinsky or the latest Warhol. But when it comes to throwing darts at it, remember what will happen to the wall behind it; pick up your walking-stick; call up your dog, and go off to a pub where a dartboard looks really at home and the tiny hush greeting a man trying for a final double sweetens the drinking delectably.

They reckon, those who make it their business to reckon such things, that darts is far and away the most popular game in a pub. From time to time there have been think-pieces in newspapers and magazines running rather pointedly short of forward-looking material forecasting the imminent decease of the game in favour of David Frost or do-it-yourself striptease or whatever is the fancied ploy of the moment. Each new forecast seems to galvanise the game into new life. This is especially pleasing to Mr Sydney Marks, who is the boss of a firm called M. Y. Dart (Games) Ltd of Barnet in Hertfordshire. Confusingly or appropriately, the firm of M. Y. Dart (Games) Ltd have a strong line in dartboards and darts. The latest figures I have seen speak lightly of an output of twenty million darts and two million boards a year.

It is true that, because of an insatiable desire of people in what used to be the British Empire (and, for my purposes, that includes America) to re-create the ambience of an English pub in torrid clime or mountain glen, something like 80 per cent of this formidable output goes abroad. But the quickest of calculations indicates that this still leaves 400,000 dartboards and four million darts for what is oddly called home consumption each year.

Those reckoners reckon that about four and a half million people in Britain play darts. I do not know how they arrive at such a figure, but everyone loves a good solid statistic, so let's not quibble. Certainly the figure for those who *have* played darts at one time or another, and will be seen to be playing darts at some time in the future, must include pretty well every drinking male in the country and more than several lady sippers. For the whole beauty of darts is that the merest beginner can enjoy a game; and yet to see a champion at work is to witness a small miracle. There are few games whose gamut of pleasure is so wide.

As with so many of the best English institutions, no one is really certain how old the game of darts is, or exactly how it began. It's a fair guess that it's a wet-day or indoor version of archery. Some claim that it began with shooting light arrows at the business end of a tun of beer or a barrel of wine. Others that weighted hand-arrows, about a foot long, were flung at mini-archery butts. Most experts agree that as a pub game it was dying out before the First World War, but revived with amazing alacrity between the wars. Bored soldiers in canteens used to play it, and brought back the habit with them, as they did with Woodbines and corned beef. For good or ill, all three have survived.

Again, as with so many of the best English institutions, the game only *seems* complicated. It has, in fact, the sort of simplicity that goes with the true aristocrat.

The board, for instance. The board we all know and love is sometimes called a clock: that is because it is nothing like a clock except in the most sketchy way. Anyone who thinks a clock is something that reads 20.11 when every respectable timepiece is saying 12.45 has been going to the bar too often instead of paying attention to the game.

Where, in fact, 12 would be in a clockface the dartboard has 20. The reason why 20 is at the top is because it is excessively difficult to aim a dart successfully at the zenith of the board. It is even more difficult to get your dart in the outer ring by the figure 20, and incredibly more difficult to get your dart into the tiny inner ring between the figure 20 and the centre of the board. The outer ring counts double, and that inner ring counts treble. It is easier to get your dart into one of the two centre rings than it is to get it into the treble-20 ring. The proof is that the inner central rings counts 25 and the dead centre, the bull's eye, counts 50. As you try unavailingly to get your dart into the 25-inner or the 50-bull's-eye or the 60-treble-twenty, you may well wonder by what standards these fine shades of difficulty are measured. The reckoners say so, and that is that. That has, in fact, been that for so many years it is now part of taproom writ; and you go against that sort of wisdom at peril of life, limb and sanity.

The very centre of a dartboard, the absolute eye of the bull, must be exactly 5 ft. 8 in. from the ground. It has been said that this represents the eye-level of the average Englishman. This is not to reckon on the reckoners: in this case insurance actuaries, who spend their lives assessing men's weight, height, girth and much else besides. They reckon that the bull's-eye is very slightly above the average man's eye-level, which shows how our ancestors looked after themselves. For the successful dart trajectory is not a bee-line flight, but a gentle arc, travelling up from the wrist and hitting the target on its downward path from orbit. One of the most successful dart players in the game's history, Mr Tom Barrett, was 5 ft. 8 in. high when he established a record by winning the *News of the World* darts championship twice in successive years. That means that the top of his head was level with the bull's-eye: a gentle trajectory, remember . . .

Mr Barrett, a compositor with Odhams Press, achieved

his championship double in 1964 and 1965. All reputable games of darts call upon the player, either as an individual or as a member of a team, to score 301, 401, or 501 points, always finishing on a double — the outer ring of the board or clock. The sort of game I play insists on starting on a double, too — but championship matches tend to allow you to score right away with what you throw.

The highest possible score, using the traditional three darts per 'throw', is 180 — three treble-20. Playing in matches, the really crack players are content with less — though unlike fun players they all have a liking for the 20-slot. Unlike my darts, theirs never seem to lose length on the way to the board and end up with a 3: a long way due south of the compelling 20.

When Mr Barrett needed to score 501, he was liable, in match play, to get it something like this:

No. 1 Throw: 100 (2 double-20 and a single 20)
No. 2 Throw: the same
No. 3 Throw: the same. Is the man human?
No. 4 Throw: Yes he is. Score 87
No. 5 Throw: He now needs, as reckoners will already have reckoned, a score of 114 to finish. He gets it with a treble-20, a single 18, and a double-18.

Five throws, 15 darts.

There's nothing to it, really. On another occasion, he got his total in four and two-thirds throws — fourteen darts, starting with a score of 135 and finishing with a score of 72, accomplished with the first two of three darts: a treble 12, a double 18.

Before Mr Barrett's time, the recognised ace was Mr Jim Pike. Mr Pike played darts with such constancy that he wore a groove in the third finger of his right hand, the one over which the shaft of the dart travels on its arcing way to the board. He once finished three games of 301-up in two and a half minutes. He also went round the clock scoring a double in each section in three minutes thirty seconds. The historian of this particular achievement noted that he threw from a mark of 9 ft — the standard mark or 'hockey' is 8 ft — and retrieved his own darts between throws. There was nothing of the prima donna about Mr Pike.

All the same, there is something about darts, more than any other pub or club game, that brings out the record-making itch. The *News of the World* national championship had its twenty-first birthday in 1968. A quarter of a million aspirants enter for it each year.

To start with, these competitors knock each other out, as it were, on their familiar home territory: their own pub or Club. The stars gradually work their way up through House Champion to Area Champion, and then to Divisional Winners. It is the eight divisional winners who compete in London for the national individual championship. To start with, the *News of the World* sensibly allows the early games to be played according to local rules: there's nothing like an importation of a foreign element into traditional rules to create a divided house of even the best mannered public bar or snug. The only thing they insist on is that the games shall be 501 up. But when it comes to area finals and beyond, then standardisation sets in, and we confront boards that are exactly 18 in. across, with $\frac{1}{4}$ in. bull's-eye radius and the double wire nearest to the centre being exactly $6\frac{1}{4}$ in. away. And so on. Such micrometric accuracy is essential when you get players who, just for limbering-up, have been known to pierce a cigarette in someone else's mouth and impale it with accuracy on the dartboard behind the victim. At this stage darts becomes a fierce encounter. Indeed, ferocity is the word chosen by the experts on the *News of the World* to describe their competition. Why, they say, the 1967 champion was actually knocked out in the quarter finals of the Eastern Counties Divisional Event the following year; and the chap who slew the giant didn't himself get as far as the Grand Finals.

I find myself at this point feeling slightly disapproving. Darts at this level has moved out of the pub and into the great halls — Alexandra Palace for the finals, no less. Pub games ought to stay in pubs, although I can see the difficulty if the *News of the World*'s championship were to be resolved in, say, the Swan Inn at Parsons Drove in the Isle of Ely, or the Waterloo Hotel at Darlington, to name but two hostelries that have lately nurtured champions. I mean, where would the television cameras find room?

Luckily, champions, runners-up, finalists — all revert to being pub players. They know that when it comes to darts the proper accompaniment is beer and not flood-lighting.

A champion darts player may go into training before a big event to keep himself in trim. Mr Barrett, I believe, used to skip to keep himself fit. He is on record, however, as saying, 'I usually have three or four brown ales before a match and another two or three during it. I don't find it affects my game.'

The beauty of darts, as with nearly all good pub games, is that a very good player doesn't have to match himself against another very good player to enjoy the game. Most ball games — football and squash rackets, for instance — are ruined if the opponents are widely different in their class of play. And although it's a bit dispiriting to be always beaten, at least a champion's opponents do get a throw, and can learn a thing or two by watching how he balances at the mark, sights his dart, draws his hand back until the dart flight is near the ear, and then throws with wrist loose and good follow-through.

In team darts, however, it doesn't always pay to have a champion on your side. After Mr Barrett's local, the Brown Bear at Hanworth in Middlesex, had headed a local league ten years running, the other clubs packed it in. One can see their point.

If you can't field a champion on your side, the next best thing is to have peculiar local conditions. I once played darts at a pub in Great Rissington which had a dartboard grey with grease, illumined (if that is the word I seek) by one smoking oil-lamp about six inches away from the 13 slot. The locals had developed a special muscular contraction of the eye which enabled them to play a fairish game. For all others the temptation to leave the mark and walk to the board peering for the double-19 was almost irresistible.

That particular board was made of something that must once have been bristle, as many better boards are to this day. Others are made of wood or rolled paper. One dart-board made of used matches — 26,673 of them — was made by a patron of the King's Arms at Hartland in North Devon. At one time all darts were wooden with a metal point and feather-flights: the best feathers for this purpose came from turkeys, it was said.

These were the sort of darts that would be handed over to you by the landlord if you asked for a set: casually kept point down in a handy tumbler by the till. Now darts tend to be heavy metal affairs, streamlined, carrying plastic or paper flights. Dedicated dartsmen, those who play in teams, keep — indeed, treasure — their own darts. Some file the points to needle sharpness, and change flights for each game.

You can play the standard game in every pub; but regulars frequently play variations on some well-known variants, such as Cricket (a bull's eye is two wickets), Shanghai (a vicious knock-out game that brings out the worst in otherwise humane players), and Round-the-Clock ending in the bull. And even more difficult are surviving non-standard boards. Timothy Finn, in his excellent *Watney Book of Pub Games*, describes the York-shire Board, which has no trebles and no outer bull, and the Staffordshire Board, which is a Yorkshire Board plus two small extra scoring areas — 25 a time — high up to the left and right of the boards.

There is also talk of clay boards in the remoter Mid-lands, where wooden darts are obligatory.

Scientists have — there being nothing sacred — studied the mystique of darts. One such, a space physicist, 'with the help of an electronic brain', decided that the left-hand side is the 'optimum sector', giving the best chance of consis-tently high scoring. The views of Mr Pike and Mr Barrett on such an incursion into their territory are not on record.

PUB

It would not be surprising if, somewhere at this very moment, a scientist of sorts is seeking to probe the secrets of optimum energy as applied to the shove ha'penny board.

As a shove ha'penny addict, I'd prefer him to turn his attention to something useful, like getting drink stains out of a Christmas morning tie, rather than interfere with our secret skills.

It is not really part of our hauteur as we bend over the board that we shovers of ha'pence should remember the distant past of our game.

At the very time, give a decade or so, that Henry VIII was encouraging darts because it was a game that did not interfere with archery, he was also promulgating a degree banning the game of shovegroat because it did. A century later, some busybody, in the way they have, dug up this old law — uncaring that the gun was replacing the arrow — and clobbered a Westminster innkeeper to the tune of ten shillings.

But groat or halfpenny, the shovers of England continued to shove in defiance of the law. To this day it is not wise to fall foul of a shove ha'penny expert in full shove.

At one time there were two versions of the game, one of them the version we know, more or less, the other played on a large board with discs. This evolved into shuffleboard which is not played in pubs.

Nowhere is the British instinct for leaving a good thing alone better exemplified than in the game of shove ha'penny. As far as can be told, the game today as played in pubs is substantially the same as that played 400 years ago. Henry VIII was keen on it himself at one time until he lost money steadily to better players, then he gave it up and made everyone else give it up too. Archery? It sounds more like royal pique to me.

The idea is that each board is divided into nine sections or beds, and it is the object of the game to shove, push, or lightly tap five coins in turn until eventually a player has placed three coins in each bed. If he puts a fourth in that bed, he either knocks it out smartish with one of the remaining coins (if any) or gives a point for that bed to his opponent. Sometimes arguments break out over whether a coin is or is not properly in the bed — that is, clear of the dividing line. To solve this, some boards have hinged wires marking the lines. By lifting the wire, it can be seen if the coin is touched by the wire or not. But in most pubs a rather more pragmatic attitude is taken: if you have to look, it isn't in.

Sometimes, as in the game I play, there is a local variation which stipulates that the last coin home must not merely be clearly in the bed but must be absolutely central between the lines. This is rather more difficult than it seems, and gives a trailing player many a chance to catch up with his scoring.

Boards are made of tough wood — often mahogany or teak — or of slate. Slate boards are easy to clean but lack the subtlety of your wooden board, which has probably had beer spilled on it in the course of an evening's play. A drop of beer spilled deliberately can bring a speeding coin to a full stop; this is not only considered foul play, but is also a waste of beer.

Coins are gradually giving way to manufactured brass discs. These are all very nice and a Sign of Progress; but the quirky behaviour of real halfpennies polished to smoothness with the years is one of the pleasanter hazards of a fine pub game.

Iron Age man played dominoes, and so did the ancient Chinese. Yet the game appears to have been unknown in

England until the end of the eighteenth century. It came to us via the French, who were busy at the time with their Revolution: possibly it travelled in a refugee's dressing case. It was taken up in two very different places with remarkable gusto: in the nursery and the taproom. In both surroundings it has flourished, because it isn't noisy and can go on for hours. The most popular form of the game is called Block. To watch four oldsters shuffle the twenty-eight pieces or bones — which once were beautiful ebony with the values picked out in gleaming white painted dots, and are now almost certain to be plastic — and then proceed to block each other's progress by skilful placing of their dominoes is to observe a small work of art. A player who is thus blocked signals his failure to play by knocking with his knuckles on the table. This is often the only sound that is heard apart from the rattle of the bones as they are shuffled at the start of each new game. Good dominoes players in a good public house don't even raise their voices to order their beer. A raised finger will bring the bar man over with the drinks. Dominoes bring out a respect for the old.

Some mining villages play dominoes for quite high stakes — £1 a time, for instance — and such a habit very nearly got dominoes barred under the Gaming and Betting Act. Luckily, Labour M.P.s realised that there were lots of votes that would never come their way again should that be allowed to happen, and it wasn't.

Another fascination that dominoes possess is that the game looks so easy. There are, you'd think, only a limited number of ploys. That's what another bright scientist thought. He fed 700 instructions into a computer — more than enough, he reckoned — and prepared to show those human slowcoaches how the game really should be played. The computer was at once beaten by two dominoes players from the Bird in Hand up at Hampstead — a victory as famous in its way, when you come to think of it, as Waterloo which was won on the playing fields of that grammar school near Slough.

As quiet as dominoes is the game of cribbage, a card game with an intricate scoring system. Any observer of the pub scene will have noticed the rapidity with which crib players not otherwise noted for brain-power can calculate their scores and move these pegs around. A poet called Sir John Suckling, a noted taverner, invented the game, so it is said, in the seventeenth century, and thereby did himself a bit of good. For he introduced the pastime to rakish gaming clubs without telling anyone that his own packs of cards were marked. John Aubrey, a later chronicler, said that Suckling got £20,000 by this way, which is considerably more than he would get for his verse, as any poet will tell you. It would be nice to record that he came to a sticky end for his malpractices: but the reason he killed himself at the age of thirty-three was not guilt at his cardsharping but because he tried to free the Earl of Strafford from the Tower of London and failed.

For many years cribbage had a soiled reputation from its association with high gamesters; but it has now settled down to a respectable old age as a game for the corner table in a nice snug where there's a cheerful fire and the beer comes in pewter mugs.

Of course, nearly all card games are played in pubs; but I tend to agree with Timothy Finn, that cards is not so much a pub game as a game played in pubs. Not so with bar billiards which, as can be seen from its name, was invented to be played in bars and only in bars. A bar-billiards table out of a pub or club is as out-of-place as a suffragan bishop at a strip revue. The extraordinary thing is that bar billiards was not invented for an English pub, but for a French bar: it's yet another importation like champagne and camembert for which we have to thank the Gauls. The beauty of bar billiards is that it combines the skill of billiards with the thrill of skittles. Yes, I know that the object of the game is *not* to knock the pins down but to pot the ball: at the same time the gentle toppling of a struck pin has its moments, especially when it's your opponent who is in play. Because bar billiards could go on for ever, there's a clock-like arrangement which brings the game to a stop after the lapse of five or ten minutes. This by a blissful coincidence marks the time it takes to finish the drink ordered on the previous game. This is true whether the clock is fixed for five or ten minutes: such is the flexibility of your pub game players.

Skittles is firmly associated, as a game, with pubs if only because that splendid summing-up of all our ambitions, 'life isn't all beer and skittles', comes from a famous book called *Tom Brown's Schooldays*. In fact, that phrase is only a hundred years old: the game of skittles is probably one of the oldest in man's sports-chequered history. To quote Timothy Finn, 'Crudely fashioned sets of Stone Age origin have been found in several parts of Europe, and Ancient Egyptian graves containing skittling pins to cheer the dead on their last journey date back as far as 5200 B.C.'

In the Dark Ages, by using the nine pins as representing the demons of hell, monks sought to inject what we would call religious propaganda into the game; but, as later attempts by hearty parsons to infiltrate homely pastimes have so often proved, the pub-gamer likes to have his categories clear. Is he playing skittles or is he praying? Well, then . . .

The game had become secular enough in the Middle Ages for it to be banned — great spoilsports were those early monarchs, given a chance. From the reign of Edward III on, various laws were passed which obliged the constabulary, such as it was, to hound skittlers from their alleys. It was no good. A skittler soon learns to treat obstreperous constables with contempt, and so it was that by the middle of the sixteenth century the laws banning skittling were gathering dust in the scriveners' outhouses. Henry VIII, an over-keen shove groatist as we have seen, took up skittling too. Perhaps he imagined all the pins to be simulacra of Papal agents.

The trouble with skittles is that it takes up rather a lot of long, narrow space. For that reason you have, as it were, to go out of the pub proper to play it, even if the alley is still on licensed premises. I cannot, myself, work up much enthusiasm for this form of skittles, seeing it as an outdoor game which has come indoors by chance and is still a hell of a long way from the bar. Still, the game has devoted followers in the West Country, and at certain famous London inns like the Freemasons' Arms at Hampstead and the Black Lion at Hammersmith, which comes in fairly prominently into *The Water Gipsies* by A. P. Herbert.

The great spherical objects that one trundles along the alley in the hope of achieving a nine-pin strike are called cheeses because they look like those old-fashioned examples of the cheese-making art from Cheddar or Wensleydale. The best ones are still made of lignum vitae and weigh between 6 and 9 lb. The old-type pins weigh 8 lb, and the chap who replaces them on their metal plates is called a sticker.

Some pubs have their own bowling-green attached to their premises, and all the solemn ritual of rubber-covered shoes, magisterial gestures from the skip, and agonised contortions from the bowler *willing* his wood to go just so, can be watched from the comfort of the bar windows. This is the Flat Turf game. A rather superior version called Crown bowls, where the greens rather than the woods are biased, is also played at some pubs. A notable venue for crown bowlers is the Sun at Putney.

I am sure all these taverns and all the folk who frequent them for the purpose of skittling or bowling, are first-class examples of both pubs and players. It's just that I like my pub games to be played inside the pub. Fresh air is a fine thing for bowlers, and all that fluorescent lighting is kind on skittlers' eyes. But I can get my fresh air without going to a pub, and I have quite enough fluorescent lighting at my office to last me through the evening and the weekend. So I am sorry that what sounds like a magnificent game called Daddlums doesn't seem to have made the progress it should.

Daddlums appears to have originated in Suffolk and, as is often the way in such matters, has taken root in parts of rural Kent. It is a sort of indoor skittles. To quote an expert who watched it at the Vigo Inn at Meopham, 'Daddlums is played on a long table like a small skittle alley, at waist-level. There are nine boxwood pins and three cheeses rather like flattened doughnuts.' As the Daddlums tables are all made locally, they vary from pub to pub; and the wise daddler sticks to the table he knows. Never trust a foreigner, say the men of Kent, particularly those from the next village.

A onetime landlady of The Vigo put the appeal of Daddlums neatly. 'It's a cheery, noisy game,' she said, 'and its boisterous spirit seems to set the tone for the tap-room as it used to be.'

And there it is. Pub games fall into two categories. Those that are splendidly noisy, like Daddlums or Aunt Sally, played mainly at Oxford by hurling 18 in. batons at

6 in. dolls ten yards away; and those that are blessedly quiet, like dominoes or crib or shove ha'penny. Occasionally the demarcation lines break down: the noisy players hush at a key point, or there is a sudden outburst of profanity from that nice bespectacled man playing shove ha'penny. But generally speaking most pubs most of the time offer a bit of each. It is just as well. For one thing a study of pub games teaches one is that the all-rounder is not encouraged. It is against the laws of man and nature for a crack darts player to win at bar billiards too, or the victor at Knur and Spell as played in the North to be a dab hand at Toad-in-the-Hole as played in Sussex. Stick to what you're good at is the lesson of pub games. Muck in for a friendly, certainly; but to gain the respect of your fellows develop a little special skill.

At least, that is what I tell myself. There's a chap called Russell Cook who is one of the better shove ha'penny players in the county of Surrey. I have beaten him once; I have, once, beaten him twice; if I could beat him three times running, I would walk with a lighter step. That day, too, Ernie might come up for me with an anonymous £25,000. The point about pub games is that there is always hope. That is what they are there for.

She was nuts on public houses, was England's Virgin Queen. There's scarcely a pub of any attractions within ten miles of London that she does not seem to have looked in at, or stopped at, or slept at, some time or other. I wonder now, supposing Harris, say, turned over a new leaf, and became a great and good man, and got to be Prime Minister, and died, if they would put up signs over the public houses that he had patronised: 'Harris had a glass of bitter in this house'; 'Harris had two of Scotch cold here in the summer of '88'; 'Harris was chucked from here in December 1886'. No, there would be too many of them! It would be the houses that he had never entered that would become famous. 'Only house in South London that Harris never had a drink in!' The people would flock to it to see what could have been the matter with it.

JEROME K. JEROME

Three Men in a Boat

❁❁

There may be those among us who never play crib, never turn a domino, never throw a dart. We have never met such a person but our research department assures us they exist.

But there is one game that is played in every pub by every single customer. It is not merely the greatest of all pub games. It is also our true national pastime. I refer, of course, to Pubmanship and we are fortunate to have with us Mr Stephen Potter, the greatest living authority, to guide us through these notoriously dangerous waters.

Stephen Potter

‍‍‍

PUBMANSHIP

Basic

Few places lend themselves more readily than a good pub to the enjoyment of the rewards of sound lifemanship. Its basic rules are here clearly demonstrated. Be one thing or the other. Decide on your character and stick to it. Remember that there is a defence to every ploy, and that every gambit has its counter.

For instance, a younger man, a recently qualified chartered accountant, or the conductress of a small orchestra, may say, 'I'm afraid I'm not really a pub person. I've never had anything to do with them. They've never been in my ambience' (using a putting-off semi-French word).

'Oh I don't know,' one can reply, with a warm smile if possible. 'I understand you spent a good many hours in pub doorways strapped in a pram. You were waiting for your parents.'

For those who wish to excel in the pub world, the first question to ask is personal. 'Am I a pub man or not?' If the answer is Yes, remember to go about it quietly. It is the non-pub man who gives the volume control a half-turn upwards as soon as he enters the pub doorway, and a half-turn down to his wit and intelligence. Natives to the scene should go a little bit impersonal at the start of a session. Order your first drink with the noncommital air of a student buying a collar-stud. Never use the surreptitious voice suitable to an enquiry for a laxative in a chemist's shop. The faintest touch of breeziness is even more objectionable, or a meaningless rubbing of the hands, or the word 'well' or the slightest reference to the weather stand a man in ill stead especially if he screws up his eyes, opens his mouth, and looks critically out of the window.

Basically, the pub man will not ask for a drink in his own local. The landlord will know what to give him and how much. His manner to start with should be reserved and straightforward. At this stage he will speak to nobody, and may immediately start reading a sheet torn from a newspaper. About 11.45 a.m. he can raise one finger, not more, to a friend of at least five years' standing on the other side of the bar. Later in the day his genius for friendship may be given a freer rein; but before noon he will not notice or even recognise as his own species non-pub man who may be saying, 'I wonder if I could possibly have a small gin and tonic', or 'I wonder if you've got such a thing as a tipped cigarette?'

Basic also is the fact there there is a type of drink which is suitable for your character. This rule can be broken a thousand times but remember that a Gin and Tonic who behaves like a Brandy and Soda and yet drinks gin and tonic must start by faintly alienating sympathy. A very young man, pale, with sandy hair, should not attempt, if slightly built, five pints in a session, as if he were drinking for a bet. Women must quickly learn to strike the balance in their choice between the too manly and the too stickily feminine.

One more basic decision you must make. Saloon or Public. This distinction has a tendency to die out. My advice has always been — hang on to it. If there are social differences, emphasise them. If you are a Public man, and Saloon are in sight, look straight through them. If Saloon puts his head round the corner, look the other way. 'You haven't seen Boskin by any chance,' Saloon may say. Do not reply. By contrast Public, entering Saloon, may be easy, confident. If he is capable of thereby suggesting patronage, Saloon can offer Public a drink.

If you, a Saloon man, coming into a strange pub, cross over to the Public, because Saloon is not only empty but looks as if it hasn't been used for years, or because there is no visible service, or to save twopence, skill is needed. You may be up against two farm labourers living rent free, beautifully shod, and probably aware of the fact that they are earning double your income. Stick to your guns and ask clearly for a mixed vermouth.

If you have already had a drink at three previous pubs on your route you may, in the Public, feel like breaking the ice. I always use the same method here. Take the precaution, as you enter the town, of noting the name of a road — not a main road — on the outskirts. Then say in a relaxed way if possible, 'I'm rather a stranger here. I wonder if anybody knows Anderson Avenue.'

There will be silence.

'Anderson Avenue?' repeat, pretending to look at a crumpled envelope.

At this point the oldest and most roughshod person present may call out in a high voice, suddenly, 'Anderson — up by the police station.' One has the impression that this man has not spoken for some days. Immediately there will be a disagreement — soon a volley of voices.

'He doesn't want Anderson *Road*.'

'That's a dead end.'

'Which way are you going?'

Soon an argument is started, into which you yourself can join, particularly if you have merely invented the name. You will be one of them. Ethnologists should note that a similar opening gambit in the Saloon gets poor results.

The good pubman should be careful of what he wears. The ordinary principles of clothesmanship apply. When meeting your friends, for instance, attempt to wear the opposite. On Sunday morning at the Grapes at Old Soking, for instance, remember that Dobbs, the sidesman, making a quick detour from church on the way home, will be wearing church clothes. Be particularly tweedy. Look as if you've left a gun in the boot of your estate car. In City pubs, by related antithesis, a bowler hat and a virgin umbrella are snide wear for the Public.

Some of the worst mistakes in dressing are made by side-door type pub visitors. The Off Licence of your local opens at 10.30 a.m. By a hundred to one chance you have nothing to drink in the house. You realise you must creep out and get a quart bottle of beer. *Do not wear creeping-out clothes* . . . Discard old brown pullover with hole in middle of back. Do not have long dark hair revealing funny bald patch. Do not have shoes without laces. Be careful to put on socks — unexpected bare ankles are frightening to children. On the contrary, dress carefully in heather mixture good suit. In Off Licence enquire for impossible wine which Off will never have heard of. When settling for pint bottle of beer, do not conceal it but walk holding it up to the light, as if you were a beer examiner or brewery taster. Be still more careful if slipping in for a quarter-bottle of whisky at 7 p.m. Better in this case, perhaps, to fling on a dinner jacket. If finances allow, do try and buy beer and quarter-whiskies two at a time, to give impression of having cellar.

Why do you go to which pub?

Once the general principles have been absorbed, the pubman is free to develop his natural talents. Ask yourself why are you actually going to *what actual pub?* I do not refer to casual reasons, like wanting to sit down, proving to yourself that you have in no sense fallen for the bosom of the new girl behind the bar, pleasure of drinking, or foolhardily wanting to know if old Bloodmore remembers that you owe him two twelve six.

It may be because you want to be alone. Perfectly O.K. this — can be admirable, rather dignified. But it must be remembered that there are one-up and one-down ways of being alone. One-down is to be lonely. In Saloon especially, look occupied. Suggest that executives and assistant editors have been streaming through your office all day, waiting for a sign, hungry for guidance. You 'must relax', if only for ten minutes. Be reading *Financial Times*, but Art and Criticism page only.

A few do well by actually looking lonely, and uncared for. 'I wonder who he is?' This verges on the oft-asked question, 'Should one be an alcoholic?' The answer is No; but many otherwise completely uninteresting people do well by being a dummy or semi-dummy alcoholic. Semi-dummy comes in suddenly five minutes after opening time and takes his accustomed seat at the end of the bar. There he is again, they say. You'd never know he was a drunk. Yet the hair — that slightly wet look. He is gentle — women say it is horrible but that he is rather sweet. A big glass always full. But how often is it emptied? That is the secret of the semi-dummy drinker. He speaks seldom. But there is an age of suffering behind the words.

The Second Reason for going to a pub is social. You go to see friends, or you take a friend.

You bring a friend to your own pub, and your one-upness here is to show that your pub is better than his. You can start by building up the landlord. He is a Major

— double D.S.O. — who got out of the army at the first possible moment because his lifelong ambition had been to own a pub. Or his wife was well known in musical comedy, hence the really extraordinary series of signed photographs from unbelievable people like Shirley Temple and Seymour Hicks. Or he owns a race horse. Or he has a double Scotch before breakfast.

Or you wonder if 'L.P.K.' will be there, he being a man really well known, indeed, one might say famous as an M.P. once a Junior Minister, and an amusing writer who yet if you meet him is so completely ordinary that you would never think he was ever really a particularly remarkable man at all, thus proving that only lesser men produce weighty impressions.

Be an expert

But to build up a lasting position in your pub you must have decided on your function, and there are few better ways of standing out than being a specialist in something even if it is quite slight, like door knockers. If your subject is known to be Unions you can say, 'You know why Cousins is *terrified*?' and nobody will like to answer. Or be somehow connected with TV or the engineering side of broadcasting, mentioning D.C. panels. An expert knowledge of drink can be implied by taking great care over a commonplace drink order, by saying that sherry should never be drunk out of a waisted glass, that stout only tastes right in plain tumblers, and that port should be poured with the left hand into a right-handed glass.

We all of us have a Saloon and Public side to our character. First one and then the other is uppermost. The real test of success is to become an expert in the Public of a country inn. You will find yourself faced with a community of super specialists. Your knowledge of

County cricket, which would be perfectly adequate in the Pavilion at Lords, will be questioned and corrected within a minute. To talk about anything remotely connected with growing things will rightly seem madness, even to the novice.

'Well, I expect this rain is just what you want . . .' This is a classic bloomer on at least three counts. It will be met by an angry silence.

Personally I like a challenge and have done well by talking about things which grow but taking a *fantastically unusual angle*. I let it be known that I am keen on wild flowers, though I sometimes confuse the issue by introducing an element of the half ambiguous, by saying that I am keen on Flora.

Now to the sound man of the country Public, wild flowers means weeds. Here is where you can put him right. Ten to one there will be pineapple weed growing in the car park of the pub. It is a miserable kind of squashed-looking mayweed without the white petals. Come in holding a piece of it in your hand.

'Do you like this one?' I say to the least responsive-looking old inhabitant. There should be a silence, or people may simply go on talking.

'If you've got a yard, there it'll be. It's only just got into the country as a matter of fact.'

Somebody may look at you.

'Great spreader,' you say.

'Oh, we know it all right,' says leader of the party.

'One of the Matricarias,' you answer, ' — matricarioides,' you add with an extra clear botanical voice. 'A sort of camomile. What do you people call it here?' Short pause for discussion.

Soon everybody will be talking.

'Old Appletops, we say.'

'No, that's Muckyjuice.' Five names are suggested not without a respectful glance at yourself. If this particular bar has been visited by the English Dialect Society, locals will make up picturesque-sounding names at random, hoping to get on the tape-recorder.

In my Saloon mood I try a sharply contrasted expert ploy. The link is language. I use, in yet another guise, my old gambit of 'knowing what the name comes from'. A friend introduces me to a stranger.

'This is Mr Corbin.'

'Excuse me one second,' I say. This is to enable me, while apparently going to the Gents, to look up Corbin in my Reaney's *Surnames* which I keep near the surface of a mixed set of objects in the back of my car. Back in the pub I return to the stranger.

'I'm so sorry, I didn't quite catch your name.'

'Corbin.'

'Ah — Corbin — of the raven hair.'

'How's that?' he says — probably quite a humble old fellow with a bald head.

'Your name suggests that there is dark hair in your family,' I say. When man looks stupefied say, 'That is the meaning of your name.'

'D'you hear that, Fosgill?' he says.

'Aha — don't ask me the meaning of *that* one,' I say, as if Fosgill meant something ugly or even obscene, as these names often do, signifying 'duck-face' or even 'cowpat'.

'Yes, dark as a raven. Corb — same as *corvus*, a crow. You'll certainly find your name in Domesday.'

I will not say that these ploys make me invariably welcome, except to the thinking. But tell a Saloon type that his name is in Domesday Book and a large Scotch is certain to be forthcoming.

PUB

The speciality may well be that you are an expert in Club Games. Speaking personally, this should suit me, as it has long been my aim, with a golf handicap of 11, somehow to suggest that it is 2. But like many men of Mixed Pub blood, I am childishly unsuccessful at shove ha'penny or darts; I have never succeeded in finishing a game of shove ha'penny with my wife, who like me is brilliant in other games fields: I have to fall back on the feeble ploy of 'being used to the long table as used in South Dorset. The one where I really found my touch was at Langton Matravers,' I'll say.

I am no more successful at darts. This is certainly partly due to the kind of *block bad luck* which makes every third dart hit the wire in such a way that the dart bounces three feet backwards. Still if you have reached the stage when you are fairly certain of hitting the board it is always possible to suggest that your dart has landed almost exactly where, according to an advanced method of accumulating points, you meant it to. Confuse analytical minds by making up technical terms and nicknames which sound as if they were only intelligible to experts. If you miss a double top by two inches, say:

'A Six and a Fiver.'

'Old Mother Wilkins' will do for a total score of three.

Having made billiard breaks of over fifty I used to make the mistake of thinking that bar ('mushroom') billiards was too easy for me even to have to try. One must have a ready answer if eight-year-olds or pregnant mothers beat you easily at this game, in spite of the fact that it is above all things a game of skill, eye and experience.

Nevertheless the atmosphere of old historical games is useful if you want to stimulate the envy of your visitor with the jolly and juicy old quality of your country local, especially English friends who come from a county where the pub atmosphere is bleaker than a Nonconformist chapel, or some place where the regulars just sit in a ring and don't talk, or look sullenly at two old men playing draughts. I used to do well in the old days when my local was the Black Lion, which not only had a famous historical character frequently on view but which specialised in an ancient form of skittles in which, instead of rolling a ball, one was supposed to throw a 'cheese' which was the shape and weight of a small millstone. In the days when I was strong enough to lift this thing up I was able to demonstrate it as a unique survival of an early sport, probably Chaucerian.

Historical pubs should be basically one-up but here again great care is necessary. Historical objects can be great conversational dampeners and this fact can sometimes be used to advantage. No harm in making out your own list of world's most boring historical objects. 'In the old innyard that stone is really an old *mounting block*,' say, pointing to some meaningless-looking bit of discarded building material. If there are dark beams inside, say, whatever the facts:

'They were only recently discovered when the modern tiling was removed. Fantastic.'

Learn a few phrases from an Ancient Monuments guide. Recommended: if oak beam has faintest sign of regular indentation, speak of a 'carved soffit'.

One must be careful with American visitors who may be, incredibly, almost as sophisticated as oneself or who may be rebelling against the constant ramming of history down their throats, or have secretly come to England in the sole hope of seeing a steam engine. Sometimes therefore their responses are out of key. If you show U.S. man mushroom billiards he will say, 'Well, of course we've been playing this for about a hundred years in the Tennis and Rackets Club. It's really Bottle Pool.' If you take him to the celebrated pub on the outskirts of London which is the special scene and provenance of a famous Dickens novel, you are showing him a 'real fifteenth-century inn'.

'There it is — fantastic. What these old walls could tell you.'

'In a way,' said my friend. He comes from Syracuse, N.Y.

'The complex woodwork of this frontage,' I said, warmly.

'Well, I suppose this actual frontage is a copy? Put up about six years ago?' This made me look more closely too.

A note on landlords

We are proud of our inns and we are proud of our landlords. The truly and deeply one-up landlord can be a man still young-looking who put his war gratuities and pension into buying a landlordship. He is quiet and self-effacing, but he knows the tastes and private lives of the regulars. He is a mixture of counsellor, diplomat and friend. Ever on the decrease now, one is glad to record, are the landlords who always end by being one-down because they make the *wrong* kind of effort to be one-up. The landlord who is too aggressively ex-service, who is both sides of the bar at once, who uses out-of-date air force slang perhaps, and if the charge is four and six, will say, 'That will cost you four and a half skins.'

The ambition of another bad old type is to make his customers feel they are extremely lucky to be allowed into his bar at all, and to be sold a drink is a mark of special favour. He is like some librarians, particularly disappointed female ones, who cannot bear to see their readers successfully finding and actually reading one of their books. The landlord form of this type is especially remorseless to strangers. Any newcomer will be made to feel that he is metaphorically stood in the corner before being spoken to. There is no sound counter to this. If, when you are standing at the bar, this landlord does not seem to have seen you at the distance of three feet, don't say, 'Excuse me' or 'Could I.' Particularly don't take out silver and put it on the bar. This is one-down in all situations. Better to stand motionless, with no expression. This will make the landlord turn his back on you while he takes his time rolling a small wad of one pound notes into a cylinder to be placed carefully into a schooner glass. But he will eventually turn round, open the newspaper, stare hard at the racing page and say, 'Now sir.' Two weeks ago I found the last remaining landlord of this type in a pub not a million miles away from D. Street, W.1. It was 10 p.m. and I asked for a crab sandwich. But I didn't eat it. The crab had gone off. I spat it out. There was no apology of course. 'Personally,' said this last of the great one-downers, 'I would never ask for a crab sandwich late at night.'

The Old Cadgeman

Sometimes, driving in the car with pretty well the whole family on board, one doesn't want to involve the whole lot of them, or fork out for expensive Cokes, if one happens to want a lightning drink oneself. The classical method of doing this is to lose the way.

'Sorry, I'd better ask in here,' you say. 'What a nice name — "The Rose Revived",' you add, to interest the children. My wife immediately spots this device and is at my heels in an instant; but the average female relation and many youths will patiently remain behind. Or one can just say, 'He may be in here — I'll get him out for you.' Who am I addressing? About whom? Nobody knows.

My old Lifemanship colleagues, who were always I fear a little outmoded even before they started, used to try endless variations on the basic old How to Cadge a Drink gambit. . . . I have mentioned my 'Did you know your name was in Domesday Book?' — an example of the quieter, more subtle method. Gattling-Fenn used to tell each member of his group, as if trying to help them, that they 'should stand the first round and then you need never stand another'. His theory was that by the time it was his, Gattling's turn, half the people would be full up, or gone.

Another method — approved by me — is to pretend some man in the public bar is a famous old character. Anybody half deaf or with some sort of boil or blain will do. Your friend will stand him a drink. You will be included.

I am experimenting with this simpler sequence:

'I say Beddisloe — what does your friend like drinking? He seems a little bit isolated.'

'No, no,' Beddisloe will say. 'I do this one. What will *you* have.'

'Well, all right,' you say, looking half-annoyed, 'Vodka Martini — but this was my idea.'

Be careful of a new suggestion, which appeals to people who like this sort of thing. Open the pub door with a bang and come in pale, rather shocked.

'I've just seen a head-on crash,' you say. 'Rather not talk about it.'

'Look as if you need a drink,' people will say. No need to mention that the incident concerned two prams, grazing against each other near the Round Pond.

Essential friendliness and good nature

How does Odoreida come in here, close friends' have often asked me. 'His methods have all the Odoreida stamp,' is all I will say here. Let me just quote this not uncharacteristic sequence. I was adapting Major Bannerby-Rickling's method with ill-mannered pub guests.

Me: What are you having?

Odoreida: Large Scotch please.

Me: Do choose your drink; but I must be allowed the privilege of deciding on the quantity.

Odoreida: That's what I was afraid of.

Essential friendliness, courtesy, and good nature are as essential to the real pubman as they are to the lifeman.

❁

When you have lost your Inns drown your empty selves, for you will have lost the last of England.

HILAIRE BELLOC

'On Inns'
(from *This and That and
the Other*)

Many men dream of a pub of their own.
Dan Farson had such a dream and made it come true.
It was not, as he discovered, as easy as it looked ...

Daniel Farson

HOW NOT TO RUN A PUB!

Many, if not most, of my happiest moments have been spent in pubs. I even ended up by running one myself, the result of a mad impulse one morning when I stood in a vast empty pub on the Isle of Dogs and thought, 'It might be fun to run a pub!'

Until then my experience of pubs was gargantuan — all on the customer's side of the bar. I have drunk in the best and the worst of them, and think I prefer the worst. I feel more at ease in the down-to-earth Public Bar than I do in the 'Contemporary' Saloon. When a favourite pub is 'done up', it's rather like a friend having a nose altered — the personality is never quite the same again. I like pubs to look like pubs as they do in Dublin; or in Leith, the dockside of Edinburgh, old and wooden, with low ceilings, open fires and severe signs which state 'Women not allowed to sit at the bar' and 'Women not allowed in after 9.50.'

I have pubbed my way through Britain, across Australia and down to Tasmania where I discovered a pub so wild that taxis refused to take me to the door. It was on the waterfront and reminded me alarmingly that this was once a convict island. Women fought on the floor, tearing each other's hair while men emptied pints of beer over the writhing bodies. An old man danced crazily to the juke-box, his hair matted with blood that had stiffened over the days. A young Scandinavian engineer, who had stepped ashore a week earlier, flushed with health, was barely recognisable. The pub was owned by a tough old girl who was supposed to have 'a heart of gold' and an 'establishment' upstairs — though I saw neither. The police tried to close the place, but she had the best lawyer in town.

Australian pubs are different from our own — more like garages, with long plastic hoses that spit the beer into the 'schooners'. The drinking is a serious affair. When I was in the merchant Navy and docked in Fremantle for the first time, I was surprised to walk, or rather shove my way into a bar that was so crowded it was almost dark. Yet it was ten in the morning and the sunlight outside was blinding. There was sawdust on the floor and I relished the Wild West atmosphere.

But some Australian pubs can be downright dainty, rather like the Australians themselves — tough on the outside, prim within. I found one near Melbourne where the Gents was called 'Adam's Boudoir'.

And I remember my dismay in Vancouver where Canadian giants staggered in from the outback with fistfuls of money and had to sit down at small separate tables while a Palm Court Orchestra played sweetly in the background. Occasionally, the monotony would be relieved when a lumberjack got up to break a chair over someone's head.

The *true* pub can only be found in Britain. It's an extraordinary institution; without it, life would not be poorer — it would be unthinkable. There are pubs to suit every taste — that is part of the attraction, but when one is shown a favourite local it is not necessarily the smartest in the neighbourhood but can seem dull, even shabby, until one senses its own personality.

When I decided to cross the Bar a few years ago, and

become a landlord myself, it was a moment of impulse, but seemed logical at the time, the culmination of four love affairs: with the Pub; the East End of London; the River Thames; and British Music Hall.

For years I wanted to live in the East End. I travelled down the river by pleasure boat making notes of any place that looked at all habitable and then there were hot summer evenings of exploration on foot down thin deserted streets cut with black shadows of warehouses, or along Cable Street where drowsy West Indians placed their chairs on the pavement to catch the last touches of the sun. At times it might have been another country.

But the very few places I found, where people could live by the water were derelict or occupied by the River Police. Londoners have this strange thing about their river on which they live and thrive. Or rather they *don't* have it. They're just not interested. And then, when I'd given up, I heard of a flat that was being converted above a barge-yard at Limehouse and with an enthusiasm that swept aside every objection I found myself on a balcony at the bend of the river at Limehouse Reach with a view that curved right down to Greenwich. I persuaded the landlady, a magnificent woman who both looks and speaks like George Arliss and controls a fleet of tugs and barges along the river, to let me lease the three floors above the barge-yard — and moved in. The locals thought I was slumming but I had found romance and didn't smell the stink at low tide or hear the din as the barge-workers scraped off the rust, or notice the occasional dead body washed up on the shore below me.

Today the houses in that street on the river at Lime-house have been preserved as ancient monuments, restored and lived in by a magazine editor, an M.P., a famous

writer and a film star. A highly tinted account in a newspaper recently said that £70,000 had been offered for one
of them. But then they were derelict and I was alone
there — and I was elated. My ambition to live on the river
in the East End was achieved and I started to explore
the local pubs in the evenings.

Already, I knew such favourites as Charlie Brown's,
really called the Railway Tavern at the foot of West
India Dock Road with its large curved ceiling and
genuine dockside atmosphere that never seems to change.
But now I discovered a wealth of music palaces with
sovereigns of their own like Queenie Watts who gave
with the blues at the Ironbridge Tavern, or Ray Martine
who decimated his subjects if they dared to heckle him at
the Deuragon Arms.

The range of talent was remarkable. The Eastern
Hotel, at the top of West India Dock Road, where
Conrad's sea captains used to stay, had an old-fashioned
band with banjo and silver trumpet and a woman with
dyed red hair and one eye who sang 'I ain't got nobody'.
There was cool modern jazz at Bermondsey, on the other
side of the water; a hunchback with a horse who sang
cowboy numbers at the Rising Sun; beat groups; and the
usual female impersonators that the British are so fond of.

Sunday lunchtime was especially lively. The Bridge
House at Canning Town was crammed with dockers with
not a girl in sight except those on the stage who did a
striptease. The dockers cheered as the clothes were discarded and then went home to Sunday lunch. I brought
along Antony Armstrong-Jones, as he was then, who
took a photograph, but finally the people enjoyed themselves too much and the strippers were replaced by elderly
Indian fire-eaters which wasn't the same thing at all.

These pubs exploded with vitality and I felt that Music

Hall was back where it began a hundred years ago in pubs like the Canterbury Arms at Lambeth. Then they had adjoining rooms that were literally music halls, where for sixpence you could have a pint of beer, trotter bones, and the show.

Waiters served drink and artists had to conquer the din by the sheer force of their personality. Even with a microphone, it's the same with pub singers today who have to fight against the roar of the crowd and the crash of the crates. They have to be robust or fail.

There was also the excitement of seeing artists *live*, and I thought it would be ironic justice to make a television programme on the boom in pub entertainment and the remarkable local talent. We called it *Time Gentlemen Please*.

While we were making it I bought a turbo-jet speedboat which was difficult to launch as it weighed a ton. At last I found a slipway on the Isle of Dogs further down the river with a pub at the top of it called the Newcastle Arms. While I was waiting for the tide to float the boat off I noticed a large family of grubby children playing in the mud. Their father was the landlord of the Newcastle and came down to talk to me. After this I moored the boat there and walked up to the pub, if the tide allowed me, on evenings when I sped down to Woolwich or Gravesend in my search of the river. But something was wrong — not only was the Newcastle empty, sometimes I had to knock to get in. One evening I called with some friends and the landlord had to go to another pub to fetch the drinks. This seemed so curious that I asked what was happening and learned the pub was 'on the floor' and the landlord wanted to leave as soon as possible. It was known locally as The Pub with no Beer and as it was on the way to nowhere, with only three regulars, nobody was keen to take it over. It was then that I looked around me and thought it might be fun to run a pub!

I was embarking on a venture that any landlord would agree is hazardous. But my new home was around the corner at Limehouse, the Newcastle stood by the water, and I liked the pub being on two levels. If a wall was demolished one could look into the saloon as if it was a small music hall. And, I love pubs. With the confidence of ignorance I went ahead.

I contacted the broker who put me in touch with the district manager of the brewers who referred me, with some doubt, to his head office. They were surprised, sceptical, and finally intrigued by my plans. Their figures must have told them the pub could hardly do worse and they agreed to my taking it over.

Like the majority of pub landlords I was to become a tenant, buying all the beer and spirits from the brewers and keeping any profit that might be left over after the running costs had been paid. Probably I was the first so-called TV personality to become a tenant. But I followed the example of many celebrities, boxers and even the hangman Albert Pierrepoint.

One of my first decisions was to change the name. The Newcastle Arms seemed a bit silly for a London dockside pub. After moving into Limehouse, I discovered that my new home had been one of many small pubs that once were scattered along the waterfront in the days when beer was twopence a pint and twice as strong. I found an old guide book which described the pub — just a room with a couple of benches, a bare table and open fire, leading on to the balcony with the men working on the barges below much as they do today. The little pub was called the Waterman's Arms and it seemed right and obvious that this should be the new name for the Newcastle.

This was the sort of decision that was easy and enjoyable. So were my plans for changing the interior. But as far as practical details were concerned, I was a hopeless amateur. Knowing so little myself, I should have recruited a Gestapo-like staff with ruthless experience. Instead, I preferred to work with people I knew already, some of whom were as inexperienced as myself. This might have been all right with a club or restaurant, but the intricacies of running a pub demand complete professionalism.

Unaware of the pitfalls around me, I skipped ahead and the preparations for the take-over seemed deceptively simple. I learned that I had to pay a nominal rent to the brewers and a going-in fee which in this unique case was comparatively small, a few hundred pounds. Then there was a deposit to the brewers (I think that was £500) and on the take-over day the value of the furniture would be agreed on and I would have to pay for all the existing stock, usually a massive item but in this case only a few empty bottles.

Altogether I would have to pay over a thousand pounds, but some money had just been left to me and I regarded this as an investment. But this was only the beginning of countless cheque-books to cover the overheads of staff, glasses, electricity and, above all, the deliveries from the brewers. And there always seemed a mass of other extraneous items which had to be met.

This was *my* experience of moving-in but the procedure varies with every brewer and every pub. The licensing side is also highly complicated. There is far more to that sign above the door with one's name on it than a ladder and a few nails. As a tenant I had to come before the Magistrate's Court, and a pub manager also needs their approval. Then the licence comes up for renewal at the Brewster Session. When I appeared for the first time it was rather like an ancient inquisition and there was a sticky moment when the police raised no objection to the licence but pointed out that I had been fined for being drunk and my manager had a record for larceny. I looked at him aghast until the charge was revealed as theft of a beer mug from a pub in Portsmouth while he was in the Navy many years before. The dignitaries on the bench suppressed a smile and we received our full licence.

There was an acid comment in far off Western Australia in the *Commerce-Industrial and Mining Review* of Kalgoorlie, a gold-mine town that has never forgiven me for describing it as one of the most god-forsaken spots on earth. 'It is interesting,' commented the *Mining Review* coolly, 'that Mr Farson has reached his level — in a cockney pub.'

A pub, like a theatre, cannot afford to be closed for long so there was no question of it being redecorated in time for my opening; that was many dust-sheeted weeks to come. Also, it isn't done to frequent a pub while the previous landlord is still there. So I spent part of the time working behind the bar at the Ironbridge Tavern where Queenie Watts and her husband Slim gave me wise advice based on years of their own experience which I should have listened to more carefully.

Suddenly, I was hurried to the London Clinic to have a growth removed from my leg. I was lying in bed afterwards doubly relieved to hear the growth wasn't malignant and that we had kept our opening secret except for a few close friends. Then I had a visit from Queenie Watts. 'I thought you ought to know, dear,' she said, 'that *everyone* is going to be at your opening.' 'But we've told nobody.' 'Well, word has got round.' 'Do they expect free drinks?' I asked with alarm. 'Well, dear, they do rather expect a drink on the house.'

I decided, instead, to serve free bits of food and hire Chinese waiters from the Lotus House. An absurd gesture.

The change-over morning arrived and I limped along to find the brokers in front of little piles of money, for everything has to be transacted in cash. After the price of the furniture had been agreed, I handed my cheque to the brewers, the largest I had ever signed. The landlord shook hands and left with a smile, evident relief and his vast family. With pride I poured my first pint as a publican.

I spent the rest of the day coping with representatives, ordering glasses and cigarettes, shouting instructions about the furniture and pictures that were being moved in. Deliveries arrived and the manager and the new staff struggled with the barrels and learned how to fix them up in the cool cellar below.

After a hectic afternoon, I went home for a shower and a few minutes' rest and returned at opening time to brace myself against the onslaught. We opened the doors — and nothing happened. Finally one of the regulars crept in to look at us. Eagerly, I poured him a Guinness on the house. He rewarded me by pointing dramatically through the wall — 'The *Great Eastern*,' he said, 'was launched just around the corner — and sank!' Then an elderly married couple came in, and did so every night for the next few years. All our regulars had arrived. I don't know what they can have thought of us but at least we were different.

An occasional customer wandered in — and out — but the silence grew heavy and rather than catch the eyes of the barmen I wandered into the kitchen and ate a pancake roll under the impassive gaze of the Chinese. At least I couldn't tell what *they* were thinking.

Then, at eight, the doors burst open and a flood of people poured through them. The staff sprang into action, the Chinese waiters fought their way through with trays held high. A customer jumped on the stage and played the piano with gusto; the faithful Queenie gave forth with the blues and the crowd with their East End determination made it a great night.

After we closed I removed some Keep Britain White stickers from the lavatory and noticed one of the barmen having difficulty with a tough-looking customer who refused to leave. Remembering times when I'd been asked to go at closing time, I used the same soothing words — 'Now, now, now,' I said unctuously, 'You know we can't serve you after hours. The law's outside' (and indeed there were several policemen watching from the street), 'but I tell you what — come back in the morning and have a drink with me. All right?' Meekly, he shook my hand and left. 'There,' I said, turning to the bar, 'that's how it's done. I don't know why you all seem so afraid of him.' 'You don't know him, do you,' said one. 'He's a right villain.' A tough customer is exactly what he was; he's now serving a long stretch for a vicious piece of grievous bodily harm. Obviously someone didn't speak to him in the right way.

The next few months were spent in learning. Our inexperience was terrifying but if I'd known what was involved I'd never have started. To give a small example, I hired a coloured pianist who was a superb artist and singer but hopelessly wrong for a pub. The atmosphere was not brightened by layers of white dust and tarpaulins, for now the builders were in.

The brewer is responsible for structural alterations and

a manager has little control over redecoration, but the tenant has to pay for all the furniture and fittings so I not only had a say but was anxious to say it. I was lucky that the brewer's architect was Roderick Gradidge, an imaginative designer who shared my own enthusiasms.

He visualised the Music Hall saloon immediately and designed a series of arches to replace the wall that was knocked down between the two bars. He commissioned an elaborate proscenium for the stage, gilded with symbols of the Isle of Dogs and Music Hall, and rediscovered an art nouveau wallpaper of green and gold which covered one wall. We agreed on blood-red paint for the other walls but when these were finished he phoned to warn me I was in for a shock. They were glaring, to say the least, but they were meant as a background for posters and photos and I was collecting these eagerly. I filmed a television sequence in the ruins of Collins Music Hall at Islington and was given one of the old gilt mirrors before the place was finally destroyed. There was an auction for the photos and prints that surrounded the bar and I bid for a charcoal portrait of Harry Tate with his lopsided moustache, a vast coloured poster of the comedian Tom Leamore in a high wing collar and early signed photographs of Dan Leno, Little Titch, Marie Lloyd and Marie Kendall.

Don Ross, the last impresario of Music Hall with his tours of Thanks for the Memory, gave me a splendid poster of The London in 1900 with Marie Lloyd's name heading the bill in big red letters and by chance I interviewed Marie Kendall who signed another photo — 'For Daniel, My Love, Marie Kendall, 1873–1963', for now she was ninety years old. Another veteran music hall artist, Ida Barr, gave me some of her souvenirs and we put up a gigantic portrait of her at the age of seventeen beside the stage.

PUB

I heard that the Metropolitan Music Hall in the Edgware Road, the old Met, was being pulled down to make way for a road and a police station and rushed there with a van in time to save some of the plaster statues and cherubs as the demolition men brought the place crashing around me.

I wrote to friends in sport and show-business for signed photos and the biggest and busiest stars responded nobly.

The outrageousness of the bright red walls was subdued. By contrast, the Public Bar was austere with brown parcel paper on the walls and prints of the London river. I met a rigger in the West India Docks called Dick Whyte who painted riverside scenes in the evening while his children played around him though he'd never seen an art show or art-book in his life. I commissioned a long picture of Greenwich and one of the Waterman's and my hopes were more than justified. They were simple, in the best sense of the word, but with a charm of their own.

At last we were ready for another opening night. I was filming the last scenes for *Time Gentlemen Please* and it seemed foolishly modest, and bad business, not to include the Waterman's in the programme.

So the new pub was shown in its transformed splendour, the brass and glass glittering in the lights as we filmed Ida Barr singing the song she made famous, 'Oh, You Beautiful Doll', Sulky Gowers ('Here am I Broken-Hearted'), Tommy Pudding ('Put a Bit of Treacle on Your Pudding Mary Ann'), and Welsh George, the compere from the Rising Sun, once the Palladium of the music pubs before it was pulled down. Also a buxom girl called Kim Cordell who attacked her song with such personality that I knew I had found our resident compere and singer.

I liked *Time Gentlemen Please* when it was finished, but

all the same I was unprepared for the reaction the next morning. I walked to the paper shop, just in case there were any reviews, and stopped in the street to read them — they were raves! 'CHEERS, FARSON!' was the headline in the *Daily Mirror*. Later, the *Sunday Times* commented, 'In this new venture he is mining a rich vein of ore; if it doesn't give out he may well find himself setting a fashion.' This was all too prophetic.

The immediate result was a nightly invasion of the East End pubs by hordes of West Enders. This was a mixed blessing. I had never wanted the Waterman's to be a tourist pub but as we had no passing trade of our own it was necessary and inevitable. I tried to compromise with a cross-section and my only row with Kim Cordell was when she complained that a group of dockers arrived straight from work in their dirty dungarees.

'But this is a dockland pub!' I exclaimed, 'we should pay them to dress like that. We don't *want* Guards officers and debs who spend the whole evening with one half of bitter.'

In fact, usually the East Enders were immaculate. It was the West Ender who looked scruffy, deliberately dressing down for the occasion in jeans and head scarves. People pestered me for the addresses of the pubs in the programme and my friends and I were appalled when we went to them again to find the whole atmosphere had changed. We had to move further afield and keep our new discoveries secret.

But above all, the crowds flocked to the Waterman's. I doubt if any pub has been visited by such an unlikely assortment of celebrities: stars like Tony Bennett, Groucho Marx and Claudette Colbert ('Yes, I'm often told that,' she said to the woman who said she looked like Claudette Colbert), Norman Hartnell, Hardy Amies and

Mary Quant, Trevor Howard, Frankie Howerd, Sir
David Webster, Lady Diana Cooper. Francis Bacon came
with Bill Burroughs who wrote *The Naked Lunch*, Joan
Littlewood brought Jacques Tati, Brian Epstein came.
So did Cyril Lord, Lionel Bart, Lord Montagu, Lord
Boothby, Sybil Burton, Kenneth Tynan . . .

Shirley Bassey got up on the stage and sang 'I who
have Nothing' when she was unmistakably pregnant and
I gave a private party for Judy Garland on the hottest
night of the year. Garland's star appeal was stronger than
I realised and we had to form a battering ram to make a
path for her. Gatecrashers and gawpers were shameless
and when the heat was so bad that she almost fainted we
took her upstairs to the slight river breeze that reached
the balconies.

After closing time she decided she would like to sing
but my manager said it was against the law to turn on
the lights again in the saloon downstairs, with the piano.

'Oh, to hell with that,' said Garland, 'I'll pay the fines.'
But the manager was adamant and so, by the moonlight
from the river and reflection from the street lights outside,
someone started to play the opening notes of 'Come rain
or come shine'. Judy Garland listened closely, then with a
sudden snap of her fingers she spun round, faced the few
of us, and started to sing . . .

Reluctantly we became part of Swinging London. Kim
Cordell, her eyelids flashing with green and gold sequins,
was now a formidable star in her own right and set the
chandeliers swaying as she roared out the old favourites. I
rang the changes with a beat group, Karl King (who was
fourteen years old) and the Vendettas; Ida Barr who was
eighty-three; the jazz singer Annie Ross who was a
regular customer and not too grand to get up on the
stage; a Pearly King singing 'Three Old Ladies locked in

the Lavatory' and a man who banged his head with a tin tray to the tune of 'Mule Train'. Above all we depended on local talent which gave constant surprise. There was a taxi-driver who sang Al Jolson and a docker who gave impersonations of Frankenstein and singers who let forth with such inevitable pub songs as 'Bye bye Blackbird'. It didn't particularly matter if they were good or terrible. One girl who looked like a white mouse was so off-key that she was greeted with cheers whenever she appeared. I never found out if she took herself seriously. There was another girl in suit and specs, as severe as an accountant, with the unexpected voice of a drunken gravel-digger.

If all this smacks of conceit — it is a poor one! After Robert Carrier started his restaurant, he pointed to his waistline and boasted, 'Since I started Carrier's I've lost several pounds.' 'That's nothing,' I replied sharply. 'Since I started the Waterman's, I've lost several thousand.'

The truth was that I had achieved the apparently impossible — the Waterman's Arms was *too* successful!

It had become so crowded that it was physically difficult to fight your way to the bar. So when a customer did get a drink he made it last as long as possible.

Ironically, our entertainment proved too popular and people preferred to listen and then do their hard drinking somewhere else. Also, we seemed to cater for large numbers of teetotallers.

When you visit a boisterous music pub do not be deceived — watch the bar as well as the stage. I went to one recently where the entertainment is probably the best in London. The crowd cheered but hardly a drink was ordered during the last half-hour. People assume the place is a goldmine but the landlord is almost in the red.

Then our licensing laws are crippling. Not much

happens in an entertainment pub before eight-thirty and one has to close at eleven. Entertainment costs money and a few broken glasses can account for the profit on a barrel of beer. Legally it is difficult to charge an entrance fee.

The solution seems so simple — stagger the hours. This happens already in the docks and markets like Covent Garden and Smithfield which open at six in the morning. Stock exchange pubs in the City don't bother to open in the evening and country pubs stay open all afternoon on market day. So if all pubs have the same amount of opening hours why can't they use them as they wish, to suit their particular need? Music pubs, like the Waterman's, could open around eight and carry on until after midnight.

This may come in time. Indeed it must if the music pub is to survive. But any change will find me in my customary place — on the customer's side of the bar.

For I had reached a turning point in my life. I had been left a house on the shores of North Devon and decided to move there to write. I resigned my job in television and, reluctantly decided to give up the Waterman's as well. By now I knew that no one can run a pub at long distance. A new tenant moved in. I moved out. I haven't been back.

I suppose I failed as a publican because I lost money and that, by our standards, is failure. But I am glad I tried.

My pub by the river remains, and, I believe flourishes, though in other hands. I hope the three loyal regulars I inherited are still to be found there every night. I passed them on to the new tenant in good condition.

As for me, I am left with memories of evenings there — like the first Christmas when the whole pub was filled with East Enders singing the old songs spontaneously and literally dancing for joy — that I shall never forget.

5 March 1668

To Westminster; where I found myself come time enough, and my brethren all ready. But I full of thoughts and trouble touching the issue of this day: and to comfort myself did go to the Dog and drink half-a-pint of mulled sack, and in the hall did drink a dram of brandy at Mrs Hewlett's; and with the warmth of this did find myself in better order as to courage, truly.

SAMUEL PEPYS

Diary

How fine it is to enter some old town, walled and turreted, just at approach of nightfall, or to come to some straggling village, with the lights streaming through the surrounding gloom; and then, after inquiring for the best entertainment that the place affords, to 'take one's ease at one's inn!'

WILLIAM HAZLITT

On Going a Journey

'Mine's a Tristram Shandy.'

✸✸

The crowded, rumbustious Waterman's Arms would not have been to J. B. Priestley's taste. Mr Priestley prefers talking pubs, quiet and rather sleepy pubs. On the darkish side.

J. B. Priestley

'THEY ARE CALLED POBS'

For 'pobs' in the above title you must read 'pubs', for they are what the speaker, a Hungarian, had in mind. But who he was and how he came to discover pubs and what he thought about them — all this must come later. I must save something — and it is a charming anecdote — to round off this piece about pubs.

My acquaintance with pubs goes back to the years just before the First War, when I was a junior wool clerk (but already writing hard) in my native city of Bradford. My friends (all dead now) and I were only in our later teens then, but we spent many an evening in pubs. I doubt if we spent any mornings or afternoons in pubs, though we could have done: they were open all day before the First War. Some of them must have opened very early too, because on cold winter mornings men on their way to work, starting perhaps about seven, would look in at a pub for rum-and-coffee, rather in the manner we now associate with French workmen. Now we have radio early in the morning, but I think if I had to turn out to walk the dark icy streets I would much prefer rum-and-coffee.

My friends and I had very little money in those days, perhaps about as many shillings as youngsters now have pounds. (This explains why there was not all this fuss about Youth and the Age Gap then: we hadn't enough money to make the fuss worth while.) However, in those years, 1911–14, you could do very well in a pub on sixpence, and if you had a shilling you could go on a spree. This seems absurd, I imagine, to anybody under sixty-five. And there are times when I wish I could forget those pre-1914 prices. For sixpence you could buy three pints of beer or two pints of strong ale, very powerful stuff; and if you really wanted to go the pace and had a shilling to spend, then you could buy four whiskies — and very good whiskies too. At our age of course we never bought it by the bottle, but my father liked an occasional hot toddy as a nightcap — and I remember we had in the house those silver gadgets for crushing the sugar and lemon — and for his bottle he would be paying 3s. 6d. No cars of course; no television; no trips to Belgium or Spain to eat fish-and-chips; but men like my father and his friends, who loved long heated arguments, could get along nicely with whisky at 3s. 6d. a bottle. Incidentally, I never saw one of them tight, though there were always some fellows in the neighbourhood, not among my father's friends, who would suddenly go off on huge roaring binges, disappearing for days and then returning home to furious or tearful wives in a dreadful state. I don't know for certain but I fancy that this strange berserk boozing, on the part of men living in respectable suburbs, would be hard to find now, even in the Viking North.

Still remembering 1911–14, I find that we youngsters patronised three quite different kinds of pubs. The first and least favourite were the big glittering places in the centre of the city. Most of them had at least one large room that offered music of a sort. There would be a pianist, never drunk but never quite sober, banging away, and at intervals 'a vocalist would oblige'. If he was a tenor then sooner or later he would sing 'Thora', a passionate lament for some lost Northern beauty, or it might be 'Love Me and the World is Mine'. The bass-baritones, manlier fellows, came out with 'Trumpeter, what are you sounding now?' or in their deepest tones asked us to beware because 'Many brave hearts are aslee-ep in the Dee-eep'. I don't remember any comedians, nor any women singers. These pubs were not offering us all-round entertainment, as the clubs of today do, but a little music to help the evening along. However, it was not our idea of music, so we rarely patronised these places.

We preferred some smallish, snug and friendly pubs that were away from the centre of the city and at one time must have been well outside it. They might be said to be country pubs now in the town. The one I best remember, a haunt of rare souls, was called the Spotted House, not far from Lister Park, and I believe that in those days it was run — and very well run too — by two or three maiden ladies. It had a lot of fine old polished woodwork in it, and I regret to say that the last time I paid it a visit, between twenty and thirty years ago, most of this grand old woodwork, the settles and tables that shone in my youth, had vanished to make room for the bogus plastic luxury that too many pubs provided for younger customers who wanted to see everything tarted up. It is worth remembering, unless it is now far too late, that there never was anything shoddy and vulgar in a genuine old pub.

One good thing about Bradford then was that it was easy to get out of, being partly surrounded by moorland. A tram ride and then half an hour's sharp walking — and you were in another world. So there were plenty of real country pubs that we visited. Once or twice, I remember, three of us, solemn young chumps, spent the night in one of these pubs, after what seemed to us a Pickwickian kind of evening, when we mixed hot punch and gravely smoked long clay churchwardens. (But never, I think, with enjoyment because hot clay kills the taste and fragrance of tobacco.) It was all, if you like, rather silly, but I think it was better than taking pep pills to stay up all night jiggling and screaming in a basement. There were no girls of course on these occasions of ours, though that does not mean we had no interest in the sex; but our pub life was entirely masculine, and though we were only eighteen or nineteen we enjoyed our talk and such ideas as we had, and I suspect we talked better than most youngsters do today.

However, all this life was coming to an end, and soon we were soldiers. Those of us who came back — and most of my youthful friends didn't — returned to find themselves in a different England, where pubs no longer stayed open all day and everything cost more and too many young men were missing and too many women and girls would never feel the same again about life. From the autumn of 1919 to the early summer of 1922 I was up at Cambridge, and though I had one or two favourite pubs there, I did not spend a great deal of time in them, usually preferring to drink and talk in college rooms. In this respect a Cambridge or Oxford college is a kind of super-pub. It is for its convivial talk, and not for its lectures and essay-writing, that an Oxford education is chiefly to be valued.

In 1922, after turning down several academic jobs, I went to London to freelance, already married and about to become a father and with exactly £50 in the world. I read for a publisher, I wrote reviews and odd articles, I did some second-string dramatic criticism and even occasionally reported soccer matches. All this in addition to writing or editing books. I was never on the staff of a newspaper, but these odd jobs took me fairly regularly into Fleet Street, especially during the years 1922–25. I was rarely around there in the evening, except when doing some dramatic criticism, as I was often living in the country, and my Fleet Street pub time was the late morning or the lunch hour. Sometimes I joined Robert Lynd and James Bone at the Rainbow, and H. M. Tomlinson, that master of travel prose who had a goblin look, might be there too. I had great affection as well as much admiration for these elders of journalism, but I must add that Tomlinson was rather deaf, Lynd muttered in a Belfast accent, Bone muttered in a Glasgow accent, so that talk in a noisy bar was not always easy. But once communication was established, how good that talk was! It was probably in the Rainbow that Lynd said to Bone, 'James, we are now the kind of men our fathers warned us against.'

But our favourite meeting-place was at the other end of Fleet Street, the bar in Poppins Court, under the *London Mercury* office. I call it a bar and not a pub because we were always standing there and if any seats were provided I cannot remember ever using one. But I doubt if any pub ever heard better talk. From about 12.30 to 2, writers came and went: Jack Squire, editor of the *London Mercury*, and his assistant editor Edward Shanks descended from their office; Hilaire Belloc often looked in, occasionally accompanied by G. K. Chesterton; and among the younger wits were Ivor Brown, Johnny Morton (Beachcomber), D. B. Wyndham Lewis; and characters like Tommy Pope, a puckish little man, one of London's best talkers and dullest reviewers. No women of course, but somehow our wit sparkled without them in those middle 1920s. I made this point deliberately because for a long time now I have felt strongly that both in clubs and pubs mixed company is preferable to all-male sessions. Perhaps

PUB

I have changed; perhaps women have changed; perhaps we have all changed; but certainly in 1925 I was happy drinking and talking with no female in sight, except the barmaid, whereas by 1945 and onward I was glad to see women friends and girl colleagues joining the company. And any saloon bar into which husbands take their wives represents a little advance in our civilisation.

During the 1930s I spent a good deal of my time working in the Theatre, not only writing plays — and a dozen or more appeared in London during this decade — but also being one of the directors of a producing company. This work with its odd hours and sudden urgent demands sent me into all manner of pubs somewhere between Shaftesbury Avenue and the Aldwych, rarely for a leisurely hour or so and all too often for a gobbled sandwich washed down by the nearest tipple — 'Anything you're having, old boy.' In these pubs, at ease and gossiping away, were all those men whose work connects them with the Theatre, even though the average playgoer does not know they exist — I am thinking of house-managers, builders and painters of sets, collectors of advertisements for programmes, printers of bills, minor agents, hirers-out of stage furniture. What always surprised me about these chaps — or at least the more convivial of them — is that although they never earned large salaries or had lavish expense accounts, by some economic miracle they were able to call for round after round of double whiskies. What happens to them now, with booze at such a price, I cannot imagine, and it is many years since I dashed into one of their theatreland pubs, to grab a large whisky and a sausage roll before the company started rehearsing the second act. Perhaps they are all still there, at ease and gossiping away, calling now for rounds that will make a big hole in a fiver.

Because we often took our plays on short provincial tours, *try-outs*, before opening in the West End, I soon became familiar with a special type of pub only found in provincial cities. It is very much a theatre pub, and usually is the one nearest to the stage door. Its walls are covered with signed photographs of prominent actors and music hall star turns, dear old pals with a most dashing handwriting. The theatrical atmosphere in these pubs is so strong that the landlord and his wife always give you the impression that they have recently completed a triumphant farewell tour, whereas in fact they may never have been on the stage at all. Some of these pubs seem to be more theatrical than the Theatre itself is nowadays. Nipping across to one of these pubs, during a break in a Sunday night dress rehearsal, I never felt that the landlord, the landlady, and their favourite customers, would ever condescend to patronise our play, if only because their saloon bar, with all its photographs and Cheerio, Old Boy! and Happy Days!, was far more theatrical in the good old style than we could ever hope to be. Finally, after having rented or gone on sharing terms with about two-thirds of the theatres in the West End, I began to learn the tricks of the trade, and one place you will never find me in is the bar of a West End playhouse.

The Second World War, in my experience, did not offer many opportunities for discovering and enjoying pubs. Nevertheless, I made some visits to a pub the subject of one of the tiny essays in a book of mine called *Delight*, first published in 1949. Partly because I am now much older and lazier, I cannot improve upon what I wrote twenty years ago, so I give the little piece here exactly as it appeared in *Delight*:

'Just gin and tonic and some potato crisps. But the

time and the setting were important. During the blitz period, the early autumn of 1940, I was in London, collecting material and writing articles during the day and broadcasting very late at night to the Dominions and America. It was exhausting work and I was always short of sleep. On Friday afternoons I went down to an Oxfordshire village, where my wife was staying for a few weeks, and then returned to London on Sunday afternoon, to give my *Postscript* talk in the evening. I would arrive at this village on Friday about an hour or so before dinner, after which I crept to bed, to make up for the week's loss of sleep. Nobody wanted me in the house during this hour before dinner, so I used to stroll down the road to the village pub, where I would drink gin and tonic and nibble potato crisps. There was never anybody else at that time in the little bar parlour, and apart from exchanging a few remarks with the landlady I spoke to nobody. I sprawled, my bones aching with tiredness, near the tiny window, through which the glow of the evening dimly filtered; and I alternated potato crisps with gulps of gin and tonic. There was as little to see as there was to say. It was all outwardly dull, and might even have been thought depressing. But after all the dodging about and fire and madness of London, the sirens and guns, the endless hours of excited talk in smoky basements, the split-second microphone business, the telephoning and typewriting, the loud rumours and mounting horrors, the cables and wires and letters, the flaming midnights seen with eyeballs of hot brass, this solitary mild tippling and nibbling without a thought in my head, only an unfathomable sense of peace and quiet and remoteness, soared above mere content to become delight, never to be forgotten, fit to be celebrated in something better than this prose, an hour of poetry . . .'

And, if I may be allowed to say so, that was a pretty piece of writing. It explains too my taste in pubs. I tend to see them primarily as places of refreshment and refuge. It seems absurd now to mention hot summer days because they appear to have left this country for ever, but when there were such days and you had walked for two or three hours (motoring doesn't count) over a moor or along a country road, and you were hot, tired, very thirsty, how wonderful it was to arrive at a pub, preferably a small and humble pub, quiet and rather dark, a real place of refreshment and refuge! Or on a winter's night, to enter — as if it were a magic glowing cave — a tiny Snug. I shall make no secret of my prejudices. I detest pubs and bars that are altogether too commercially successful, with chaps four-deep at the wet counter, all apparently with trains to catch or bent on high-pressure swilling, as they always seem to be in Australia. I dislike pubs that are trying not to look like pubs, are so terrifically smart and tarted up that they seem to be expecting a visit from Noël Coward, Cecil Beaton and the editor of *Vogue*, and are only happy serving weak cocktails in appallingly minute glasses. Nor am I fond of those saloon bars crowded with shouting regulars, who argue with the landlord or the barmaid, all at tops of voices, about when Charlie — it is always Charlie — was last seen in there. As I don't care a damn if it was Tuesday or Wednesday when Charlie was there — and he never turns up himself to settle the argument — I swallow my drink and go. And I never find myself lingering in pubs where there is almost always a fortis-simo debate about a Cup Final or a Derby winner. No, I like quiet, rather sleepy pubs, on the darkish side, not attempting to look like the final scene of a Palladium pantomime.

But now I must return to 'They are called Pobs'. The

speaker was Alex Korda, the film producer, with whom I once worked on a film script — a delightful fellow and an odd mixture of ultra-sophistication and innocence. One evening he was taken by one of his younger directors to a first night at, I believe, St Martin's Theatre. There had been some confusion about tickets, with the result that Korda and the film director could not get into the theatre, so the latter proposed they should pass the evening visiting several pubs in the neighbourhood. Now Korda had already been several years in London, but his days and nights had been spent in Pinewood studios, Claridges, the Savoy Grill, the Hungaria Restaurant, and so forth, and he knew nothing whatever about pubs. They enchanted him, and for days afterwards he talked enthusiastically to everybody he met about these wonderful places in London where people drank whatever they pleased and talked freely to other people and enjoyed themselves. 'I think they are marvellous, these places,' he would say in conclusion. 'They are called *Pobs*.'

*Mr Priestley likes drinking in the company of women. Miss
Marjorie Proops smiles warmly on Mr Priestley. Not all men
would agree with him. They go to their local, they say, to get
away from their women. Miss Proops would have a thing or two
to say to them . . .*

Marjorie Proops

WHAT WILL YOU HAVE,
MRS PANKHURST?

There was this skinny pale girl wearing very wide white
satin trousers, a black leather jacket unbuttoned to the
waist revealing a non-existent bosom, a Minnehaha head-
band across her brow, long lank hair and bare dirty feet.
She was drinking a vodka and tonic in a pub off Shaftesbury
Avenue.

The barman said, 'Certainly, madam', when she called
for another drink. He did not appear to be surprised, per-
turbed or put out as he slid the second glass across to this
customer standing alongside two men with briefcases
and evening papers, obvious commuters who'd popped
in for a couple of quickies on the way home from the
office.

For their part, other than the kind of swift, mildly
interested glance all men give to all young females — in

pubs or elsewhere — they ignored her. As she did them, and all the other customers.

When she'd finished her second one (with remarkable speed), she nodded coolly to the barman and departed.

I asked him if she was a regular. He said, 'She pops in and out, not what you'd call a regular, you get a lot of them round Shaftesbury Avenue. Nice kids. No trouble, they don't hang about ...'

He worries about them catching their death, what with wearing no shoes and no underwear. 'Don't know what their mothers are up to, letting them go out without any shoes on in this ruddy climate, same again, madam?'

I adjusted my dark glasses and said no, I must be going, be late for the theatre. I always wear dark glasses when I go into a pub alone, for unlike Minnehaha, I suffer from the hangover of being brought up by parents who were convinced that a woman sitting alone in a pub indicated that she was, as they put it, no better than she ought to be.

It is therefore necessary to hide my guilt and embarrassment behind dark glasses, and I feel the need to explain to all the other customers that I am in this pub on my own because I am going to the theatre and my escort cannot make it until the curtain is about to rise and in any case, I came in for a ham sandwich, really.

However, none of the other customers pay the slightest attention to me (except, perhaps, to wonder why anyone wears dark glasses in a dimly-lit bar).

Women alone in pubs are no longer any more remarkable than men alone in pubs. That's emancipation for you. If Mrs Pankhurst did nothing else, she made us *that* equal. We may still earn less than a man for doing the same job but we have earned the right to drown our sorrows about it over our solitary drink and we ought to be very grateful to men for letting us enjoy this privilege.

There are, regrettably, still a few outposts where we are not able, as yet, to creep into a bar — either alone or with another female — to quench our thirsts. Not in a bar where men are quenching theirs, I mean.

There are still pubs in this country which have bars where women are not allowed to enter. These pubs (I've come across them in the North of England) have set aside special ladies' lounges, as they call them with commendable delicacy, where women can be kept out of the sight of men. Arguing fiercely in my best fighting feminist manner with landlords, I have denounced this reactionary segregation.

They prefer it this way, I am told. Who, I ask, are they? The men, I am assured. And the ladies.

Next question: Why? Because, it is patiently explained, they prefer to keep themselves to themselves.

Further probing whys result in shrugs and mutters of that's the way it is, love, we're different up here from the way you southerners are — and there seems to be a certain air of smug satisfaction that in the North, women know their place and men know how to keep them there.

Presumably this segregation nonsense is a legacy from the days when pubs were handy places for women on the make, where any woman settling herself down in a corner nursing a glass was automatically assumed to be a loose-living lady on the search for clients.

Thank goodness a woman nowadays can, at the end of a morning's battle in the supermarkets, lug her shopping into a pub, and order a revivifying beverage without courting hard suspicious looks from the landlord and speculative ones from the customers.

It is, in fact, a commonplace sight in suburban pubs: housewives easing their shoes off while they sip a Bloody Mary and check their shopping lists. Many of my housewife friends tell me they prefer to meet for elevenses in a pub for a gossip and sherry than in a café for coffee and biscuits.

There is, of course, still a hard-core of men who are convinced that no woman should be allowed to cross the threshold of *any* pub, at any time, except to serve behind the bar or do the cleaning before opening time and then disappear smartly. But those men who lean disconsolately against the counter eyeing the chattering female customers with liverish disapproval are fighting a losing battle.

After all, the history of the pub is really a microcosm of the English social history; the changing status of women is reflected in the changing image of the English pub.

Seventeenth-century females like Nell Gwynn and her mates were, I daresay, steady regulars in Covent Garden taverns. I imagine they gave as good as they got in every possible way; their conversation was, I guess, as colourful as their personalities.

They could drink their ale, use those charming Anglo-Saxon euphemisms and roust around with gusto equal to the gusto of any man. Some of Shakespeare's ladies clearly demonstrate that refinement was not considered to be a requisite of the times.

Doll Tear-Sheet in *Henry IV* didn't mince her words when she cried, 'Away you cut-purse rascal! you filthy bung, away! by this wine, I'll thrust my knife into your mouldy chaps, an you play the saucy cuttle with me . . .'

A far cry indeed from today's namby-pamby exclamation: 'Give over, George, *please*!'

The wife of Bath's conversation is peppered with references to getting tight. It's not a condition many women boast about today. The lady roisterer is a female of the past and some might think it a pity that refinement has taken the place of hearty vigour. I suspect that the really dedicated woman drinker knocks off the hard stuff in her Regency drawing room rather than expose her predilection in the lounge bar.

Another demonstration of the change in pubs — and women — is the change in their taste in beverages. Nell Gwynn and Co. liked ale. Obviously they weren't bothered about their statistics. They were comely girls, bosoms spilling generously out of their low-cut gowns, drinking man-sized jugs of beer with man-sized men.

Today's girls, keen on keeping their statistics down and their bosoms minimal, usually go in for small drinks. Maybe they simply haven't the capacity of their lusty forebears. Maybe they just figure that gin isn't so fattening as beer. Maybe it's because beer is considered to be a man's drink nowadays.

Women generally drink gin. Why should gin, I wonder, seem to be so much more feminine than beer? Or whisky? My theory is that women are adept at deluding themselves. Since gin looks like water they can pretend that by drinking innocent-looking colourless liquid they aren't really drinking at all.

It's part of the desire to appear refined, for only nice women, they keep telling themselves, go into pubs these days, not like in the old days when no nice woman would step across a pub threshold.

Even countesses and duchesses can be seen drinking gins and tonics in mod pubs and it is considered to be rather in, if you are a countess or a duchess or just a mere life peeress, to be seen leaning elegantly against the bar — with minky elbows on the counter.

I don't think the Queen has as yet been spotted with her minky elbow on a counter in one of the pubs in Victoria around the corner from her London pad but nothing is impossible in these democratic days. I wouldn't put it past Margaret and Tony, a very jolly In-couple, to nip in for a quickie now and then between thirst-making bazaar opening ceremonies.

The upper-classes are, I've found, accepted with amiable indifference by the rest of us.

I sometimes go to a pub for a gin and something with the only titled friend I can boast (just a viscountess, actually), and everyone decently ignores her, even though she looks every inch a viscountess, which is yet another demonstration of the social changes that have imperceptibly taken place over the centuries.

No forelock touching, like in the old days. No suspicion on the part of the other cash customers that she's up to no good . . . She is just another little ole viscountess enjoying her nourishing gin and bitter lemon.

Last time we quaffed a gin together in a pub off Fleet Street, we idly discussed the possibility of saving up to buy one. A pub, I mean. She'd often considered, she said, the notion of getting a nice little place along the river, something quiet and ladylike for the tweed set.

I pointed out the disadvantages, like having to work seven days (and nights) a week and all the glasses to wash up and the possibility of having to chuck out some of the more awkward elements of the tweed set at closing time and she saw that it mightn't be quite such a good idea, after all.

There are women, though, who run pubs and very capably, too. I know one in the Midlands, a blonde lady who always wears neat black and looks rather delicate in a way, but she runs that pub with total efficiency and she can put a drunk out and cope with the rowdies as firmly as any man.

She told me that the great thing is having the customers respect her. She makes sure they do.

The majority of her customers are men, but she has her regular ladies, too, and she says she sees no reason why women shouldn't run pubs as well as go into them when they feel like it.

'We're all more or less equal,' she says firmly and, 'if the women don't mind the men, I don't see why the men should mind the women.'

Only a small minority of women still regard a pub as strictly male territory into which they are allowed on sufferance. In these enlightened times, females of all ages and social levels feel entitled to push their way to the counter, pay for their round, and take for granted their inalienable right to be there.

And why not? This isn't Australia, for heaven's sake. There, thirsty ladies in that thirsty country are forced to hang around outside pubs while their menfolk enjoy convivial booze inside and the really lucky, cherished ladies consider themselves to be honoured if husband or boy-friend remembers to lurch outside with a drink to moisten parched feminine throats. We're *much* better off here.

The fact that women are welcomed here in pubs (well, perhaps welcomed is too strong a word — perhaps it ought to be endured) has made an enormous difference, not only to the male customers, but to the pubs themselves. Petticoat influence has produced a whole new school of thought about the way pubs must look to attract females.

It's sometimes hard, actually, to realise you are in a pub at all so downright fancy and trendy have they become — what with patterned carpets, chandeliers, potted plants, coffee tables and the kind of armchairs you'd be glad to have in your front parlour. Plus of course, TV and, in the most civilised pubs of all, colour TV.

There's really no reason why a woman should ever want to go home, for at home she'd have to empty the ashtrays occasionally and fold the newspapers and plump up the cushions, and of course, wash all the glasses.

If only the next step could be nurseries and playrooms (with nannies provided), you could practically dispense with living quarters at home. All you'd need would be the bedrooms and usual offices.

One of the other influences women have had on pubs is the food they now provide. In bygone days, practically the only women who frequented pubs were the rheumy old Guinness Girls mumbling away, poor souls, in dark corners, there only for a bit of warmth and shelter — or those aforementioned ladies who were there purely for nefarious purposes (though pure is not exactly what their purposes were). And in those dark days, it was a rare pub that provided anything more sustaining than sandwiches with mousetrap cheese fillings and pickled onions and perhaps a few greasy, unappetising sausages.

Now, thanks, in my opinion, to the compelling presence of women, it is possible to find such delicacies as *quiche lorraine,* frogs' legs, *boeuf bourguignon* and exotic curries in your favourite tavern, along, of course, with such nourishing staples as roast beef and Yorkshire pudding and steak and kidney pud.

There is positively no reason why a woman should bother to slave over a hot *quiche lorraine* when the chef in the pub in the High Street can save her the trouble and no one would deny that it's nicer to eat your *quiche* at a trendy marble table with wrought iron legs than at your own kitchen table littered with the shirts you've got to iron later.

Which stimulates another thought: along with nurseries and nannies, it would be nice to have some place to wash out a few smalls and rub the iron over them between drinks. Not every pub has a handy launderette close by.

But before the brewers start considering putting in washing-machines and steam irons, they really ought to take a long hard look at their existing plumbing and what are euphemistically known as the powder-rooms in pubs.

I have been in more revolting lavatories in pubs than I've had hot dinners. There's a lot of room for improvement in this particular area. Squalid little rooms with grimy towels (or none at all); dirty washbasins; slimy bits of soap; penny-in-the-slot doors; spotty-looking glasses and nowhere to park your handbag or make-up — that's the picture far too many pub ladies' rooms present and it is a sad and discouraging picture. Very off-putting. Not all the trendy marble tables with wrought-iron legs in the kingdom would make up for these nasty little hell-holes.

Women would be grateful for pretty and properly equipped facilities and I guess they'd pay off. As it is, a woman is likely to refuse her third drink, knowing she'd better get back home fast, anything — even skipping another drink — being preferable to going down a dank back stairway to the unspeakable 'Ladies'.

There is, of course, one big danger brewers and landlords face in their all-out efforts to make pubs alluring to women: the danger of alienating the men. Men, I gather, prefer lino to ankle-deep carpet: are fed-up with falling over trendy coffee tables; are totally disinterested in glittering chandeliers and only put up with potted plants because they're useful for dropping cigarette ends in. They'd rather stand until their backs are practically breaking than lounge in a comfortable armchair.

PUB

Men feel ill at ease with jazzy curtains and plastic flowers. Give them brass rails, wet counters, dirty windows — an atmosphere of beery dedication to drink with no nonsense — and they are happy.

Still, they are liable to have trouble with their wives and girl-friends if they put up any serious resistance to progress, for women are no longer prepared to sit at home and knit and watch the telly while their men go off alone to the pub. The women insist upon accompanying their loved ones and if the pub to which they are escorted fails to come up to feminine standards of comfort and luxury, the men are liable to be the victims of unremitting nagging.

Many a man has had to abandon his lovable, sordid 'regular' for something shinier and glossier and groovier, just to keep *her* quiet. It's a matter of self-defence and simple common sense, for any sensible man realises that his only hope for domestic peace and tranquillity is his ability to keep the woman in his life happy.

It therefore behoves any intelligent male to make a careful study — not only of the female to whom he is attached — but to the type of pub his particular woman would find most rewarding.

Ever anxious to be of service to mankind, I have worked out a simple guide for men based on woman types and their pub types, so that a man can do the necessary reconnaissance of suitable pubs and thereby reduce the nagging:

Sunday-morning sporting: This sort tends to wear good tweed skirts and clumpy shoes and is often accompanied by a large dog. The Sunday-morning sporting bird has a loud chirp and is often to be heard calling, 'Half-a-bitter, please; half-a-bitter, please', which she then carries back to her mate.

PUB

Her pub: Oak-beamed, with horse-brasses and lanterns, preferably a good inglenook and roaring fire. In summer, a fine garden.

Mini-clad trendy: This runs to wispy blonde hair, round mauve sun-glasses (even in winter), and skinny crochet dresses which seem to end just below the navel. She is fond of expensive drinks with lots of salad and fruit in them but avoids crisps, which catch in the crochet.

Her pub: Anything with a cocktail bar and good big windows where she can be seen and envied from outside. Preferably on a wide street where she can come out from time to time and lean decoratively against her boy-friend's Jag, clasping her drinkie.

Pay-day typist: Friday-night drinker who gathers in small flocks, often unaccompanied by males. Interesting eye-make-up and a sensible attitude to booze, i.e. lightly alcoholic drinks with fanciful names consumed with great speed and chatter amid clouds of onion-flavoured crisps. Also likes peanuts.

Her pub: Prefers pretty wrought-iron and lots of flowers and greenery, even if plastic. Top marks for pub frequented by flocks of nice young men. Avoids pubs where crisps not provided.

Housewife: Easily recognised by large, full shopping baskets and flat feet. Usual cry: 'Ahh, that's better.'

Her pub: One with large warm rooms and plenty of comfortable chairs round little tables. Copies of women's mags much appreciated.

Glossy girl with glossy job: Good suit, clean fingernails, often hatted, often with a man not her husband; drinks whisky.

Her pub: Cult pubs where barman (never barmaid) knows her. Small, hard to find pub, probably in a mews. No public bar.

In the same way that I am eager to be of service to male pub customers, I am equally solicitous towards female pub customers — especially unaccompanied ones. There are distinct hazards — or interesting opportunities — depending on the way women look at it — and the way men look to them.

Here then, is yet another simple guide. This one is strictly for the benefit of the ladies. It is a guide to assist them in sorting the wheat from the chaff, the men from the boys, the Doves from the Hawks.

The Rugger Hero: Sunday sporting women may like this one, but he is certainly a special taste. Speak to him only if you wish to spend every Saturday from 2.30 p.m. to 4.30 p.m. in the rain by the touchline, 4.30 to 5-ish consuming four cups of tea, three bath buns, three shrimp paste sandwiches and a chocolate biscuit, and five onwards in the bar standing up drinking pint for pint with your man. If you can coax him out of the rugger club and into a nice, nearby pub, you might persuade him to let you sit down.

The Know-all: Apparently made in one piece with the bar-counter, where he has buttonholed the publican with a deluge of rhetoric on politics, Vietnam, sex-and-the-young, and whether or not to use manure for roses. Even if you did speak to him, he wouldn't hear you.

The Morose Lingerer: That man in the far corner drawing patterns in the beer stains who stays till closing time on the strength of one pint of mild. Will tell you the story of his life if you so much as come within ten yards of him.

The Man with The Dog: Identical with the above, except he talks only to the dog.

The Cheerful Imbiber: Beloved of barmen and apple of brewer's eye. Buys drinks for other people. Unfortunately often apple of wife's eye, who is that stern woman there, yes, that one, with her eye on you.

The Depressed Romantic: Perhaps the most promising for a single girl. Usually drowning his sorrows, after current flame has cast him aside. Nip in quickly and she'll never get him back. Good for any quantity of Pimms No. 1 until his sanity returns.

The Sponger: Usually well dressed, fond of suede chukka boots, has frank open smile, picks housewives or career women and engages in innocent chat about the weather. Buys one round, offers second, 'remembers' he's 'forgotten' his wallet. Manages to extract several drinks, lunch and, if extra lucky, a pound or two from victim before closing time. Fails to reappear next day as arranged. Is in another pub, working the same racket.

The Intellectual: Easily identifiable: lank hair, burning eyes, several paperbacks bulging from shabby jacket. Searching for good listeners to whom he can propound his philosophy over half-a-pint. Is liable to suggest continuing fascinating conversation at his place (basement room with no furniture except a bed).

There are, as I say, pub hazards (or opportunities) for susceptible ladies who simply feel thirsty and in need of a long cool drink. It may have been noticed that I have not listed the hazards men might face in pubs. They, I feel, can take care of themselves — in pubs, and everywhere else.

I have heard it said that the cosy peace which envelops the bar-parlour of the Anglers' Rest has a tendency to promote in the regular customers a certain callousness and indifference to human suffering. I fear there is something in the charge. We who have made the place our retreat sit sheltered in a backwater far removed from the rushing stream of Life. We may be dimly aware that out in the world there are hearts that ache and bleed: but we order another gin and ginger and forget about them. Tragedy, to us, has come to mean merely the occasional flatness of a bottle of beer.

Nevertheless, this crust of selfish detachment can be cracked. And when Mr Mulliner entered on this Sunday evening and announced that Miss Postlethwaite, our gifted and popular barmaid, had severed her engagement to Alfred Lukyn, the courteous assistant at the Bon Ton Drapery Stores in the High Street, it is not too much to say that we were stunned.

'But it's only half an hour ago,' we cried, 'that she went off to meet him in her best black satin with the lovelight in her eyes. They were going to church together.'

'They never reached the sacred edifice,' said Mr Mulliner, sighing and taking a grave sip of hot Scotch and lemon. 'The estrangement occurred directly they met. The rock on which the frail craft of Love split was the fact that Alfred Lukyn was wearing yellow shoes.'

'Yellow shoes?'

'Yellow shoes,' said Mr Mulliner, 'of a singular brightness. These came under immediate discussion. Miss Postlethwaite, a girl of exquisite sensibility and devoutness, argued that to attend evensong in shoes like that was disrespectful to the Vicar. The blood of the Lukyns is hot, and Alfred, stung, retorted that he had paid sixteen shillings and eightpence for them and that the Vicar could go and boil his head. The ring then changed hands and arrangements were put in train for the return of all gifts and correspondence.'

'Just a lovers' tiff.'

'Let us hope so.'

P. G. WODEHOUSE

'The Story of Cedric'
(from *Mr Mulliner Speaking*)

There is one woman who has always been in the pub. She's still there, praise be. A pub wouldn't be a pub without her. Give thanks, gentlemen, to your friend and my friend, the Greater British Barmaid . . .

Maureen Cleave

THE GREATER BRITISH BARMAID

'*I've always loved bar work; I love people. Bar work is the next best thing to stage life.*' A barmaid.

'*If they tell me dirty stories, I tell them a few and we have a good laugh. You've got to give and take in the public bar.*' A manager's wife.

'*I think men are very soft really.*' An Irish barmaid.

'*As you know yourself, men are all animals. First and foremost in a man's mind is sex.*' A Scottish barmaid.

'*Now you see these advertisements: "No experience necessary; mini-skirts only." If something isn't done about it, it will be like Sodom and Gomorrah with vice over the whole country.*' A middle-aged barmaid.

'*When I came over, I was going nursing and my friend said, "Why not try bar work?"*' An Irish barmaid.

The barmaid is a woman in what is still a man's world — very much a man's world in spite of changed times and enticing advertisements from the brewers; in spite of dainty drinks betopped with glacé cherries for the lady customers, who lack what one barmaid delicately called 'the liquid capacity' of a man. No; pubs means beer, and the only woman with a rightful place in the English pub is the barmaid who serves it. By tradition a blowzy, saucy creature with a meaning laugh and a heart of gold, she is referred to with ribaldry, regarded with affection; jokes about her centring on her bosoms, popularly required to be large enough to rest on the counter.

But women have more to offer to the licensed victual-ling trade than these visual charms. They are vital to it. Quite often the descent of the publican may be traced through the female line. Take the case of Mrs Barnett (now married to Micky Barnett, the tenant of the Albion, a pub at the bottom of Fleet Street in London). Mrs Barnett's great-grandmother, Mrs Savage, well over a hundred years ago owned the Black Boy in Nottingham. Her grandmother, Miss Savage, married a Mr Reimers and brought him into the trade. Her mother, Miss Riemers, married Mr Graves and brought him into the trade. Miss Graves married Mr Barnett and brought him into the trade. To this day Mrs Barnett has a letter from the brewers to her husband saying, 'Subject to your marrying Miss Graves, you may have the King's Arms . . .' Now their son has his own pub.

Being a barmaid is one of the older professions with a long and distinguished tradition. From medieval times, and conceivably long before, the water of England was rightly considered undrinkable, whereas milk was held suitable only for butter and cheese; everyone, man, wo-man and child, drank ale, ale that was sterilised in the making and nutritious. And just as the housewife cooked her husband's dinner, so she brewed his ale. And as ale-houses grew up, so she brewed and dispensed ale in them. She was called a brewster.

So important was she, one might almost say that a brewer was a male brewster.

But it was not until Victorian times that the barmaid acquired social status. (There is a famous cartoon showing Queen Victoria herself in a small but costly crown on duty behind John Bull's bar.)

H. L. Beales, the social historian, in his authoritative essay on the Victorian barmaid points out that the railway was responsible for this. The first *Bradshaw* in 1839 stated that there was a refreshment bar at Wolverton station with 'a female in attendance'. In fact there were seven young ladies in the strict charge of a matron. They rose at seven in the morning and sank to their beds at midnight. They conducted themselves in a decorous manner and, as a reward, four of them contracted excellent marriages. A visiting French cartoonist was most impressed by the English barmaid. He described her as 'a kind of moral salamander, living unharmed in the midst of the amorous furnace in which Destiny has placed her'.

And today barmaids still often work in what are called 'live and sleep-in' conditions, all together. This is the set-up at the Railway Tavern near Liverpool Street station where five barmaids live together, four of whom are Irish, three of whom are called Mary, two of whom are called Mary Theresa, and at least one of whom is beautiful in an Irish way with pale skin and dark hair. They work and eat and watch television together. Their bedrooms lead off a long passage. Two sisters, Mary and Margaret Ford, share one of these with a panoramic view of Liverpool Street station. 'We were told not to keep late hours,' Mary Ford said; 'it's not necessary for a girl who's got any intelligence to be out very late at night.'

One wishes her the same marriage prospects enjoyed by the virtuous young ladies of Wolverton.

Thackeray himself wrote a pretty poem to a barmaid called Peggy at this time:

> See her as she moves,
> Scarce the ground she touches,
> Airy as a fay,
> Graceful as a duchess.
> Bare her rounded arm is
> Bare her little leg is.
> Vestris never showed
> Ankles like to Peggy's
> Braided is her hair,
> Soft her look and modest
> Slim her little waist,
> Comfortably bodiced.

Clearly a good girl, Peggy. But in the earlier part of this century the reputation of the barmaid takes something of a knock. The amorous furnace got the better of her, but in fairness bars then must have been quite disagreeable places with sawdust and spitoons and the customers practising how far away they could spit into them. Contemporary barmaids draw a veil across to the mid-thirties, at which time wages rose and the barmaid no longer found it necessary to sell more than the beer. After the Second War women began to do risqué things like smoking in public, and pubs became the jolly places we know today. Mrs Barnett can remember conceiving the daring idea of putting a carpet in the public bar in 1962; people came from far and wide to look at it.

'Years ago,' she said, 'it was all pints and pints of mild ale. Now it's more like a cocktail bar and people like a serviette with their sandwich.'

The ladies whom today we find behind the bar are of

seven sorts: there is the tenant's wife (tenants being people who rent the pubs from the breweries and who take the profits); there is the manager's wife (a manager being someone who is paid a salary by the brewers); there is the barmaid who gets a weekly wage (up to £14 a week, or £10 a week live and sleep-in; these ladies are often Irish and have sometimes taken the pledge); there is the part-time barmaid, who gets between 25s. and 30s. a session. Then you get the lady tenants and the lady managers, though these are rare. And lastly, one of the wonders of our time, the Australian barmaid.

These are beautiful, clear-eyed, healthy, athletic girls with long, bare, brown legs beneath their mini-skirts, who have given up satisfactory livings as teachers, solicitors and accountants in order to come to Europe for two years. They stop off to be barmaids in England in order to re-stock their funds. Anyone will tell you they make excellent barmaids. There is one called Ursula Delaney in the Chelsea Drugstore, that new complex of swinging activity in the King's Road, Chelsea. Miss Delaney looks just like a madonna in the face. Her father is a well-to-do butcher in Sydney, her mother an interpreter, she herself a school-teacher, aged twenty-three. She loves it. No one, she says, tries to tell her dirty stories and looking at her one is not surprised. When she does have occasion to rebuke someone she says, 'Stupidity I'll excuse, rudeness never.' And that usually copes with that.

More than most she has rationalised her approach to her work. 'I do it,' she said, 'to open up a facet of myself that has not been developed. Last week a bloke came in who said he was a painter. Well, I thought this is just the sort of garbage a barmaid has to put up with. Then I thought: it's stupid to be so sceptical about too many things. After all, I have gotten out of teaching in order to open out to new influences.'

And the happy ending to the story is that Miss Delaney is now having her portrait painted.

Her colleague is called Miss Jackie Kirkham, a very pretty girl with huge eyes and lengthy eyelashes. She was articled to a firm of solicitors in Sydney and keeps meaning to go back. One wondered how long it took her to learn the job. 'Nothing to it,' Miss Kirkham said easily. 'Here we have measured half-pints and you push a button. Each time you push a button, a measured half-pint comes out, and you push it twice for a pint, you see. The head comes out by itself. You can pick it up in half an hour.'

This is the sort of remark that makes other barmaids reach for the parallel with Sodom and Gomorrah.

It is impossible to generalise about such a diversity of ladies but one might say, at least about the older ones, that they are round rather than angular; that they are slow to anger, quick to catch on. If they wear spectacles they favour those of upswept design. And they do laugh loudly — a barmaid must not only laugh, she must be seen and heard to laugh — they all laugh very loudly indeed.

What they have all, young and old, grand and humble, in common is the problem of the beer. This makes the soles of their shoes drop off and it makes their dresses go stiff. (Hence perhaps the sergeant major's insult to his raw recruits about the devastating effects of a sniff of the barmaid's apron.) 'It looks all very nice from here,' one barmaid said from the front of the bar, 'but at night that floor is a mass of beer and bottle tops.'

And from being on them all day, they suffer with their feet. They work incredibly long hours. The barmaid usually checks in for work at 10 a.m.; often she washes the floor behind the bar; she polishes her glasses; she cleans the bottles behind her in what is known as the display cabinet. Then she works the first lunchtime session from perhaps 11 till 3, with half-an-hour off for lunch; then the evening session from perhaps 5.30 till 11. Then there is clearing up. Then, more often than not, there's a little party. Mrs Clarke of the Sparrow Hawk in Edgware said, 'We always sit down with the staff and have a little natter and a drink and a sandwich. Saturday's a very very heavy day and come 11 o'clock we have baked potatoes and perhaps some prawns or winkles or cockles — a really good feed.' Mrs Barnett and her husband go out to supper and then perhaps on to Mr Danny La Rue's night club. Jackie Kirkham goes to a club with a boy-friend. Life for the barmaid begins after the clearing up.

'You get used to feeling tired, darling,' Mrs Barnett said. 'It's not what you do; it's to know how to relax.'

Clara Elizabeth Cliffe is the tenant, with her name over the door, of the Waggoners near the hamlet of Welwyn in Hertfordshire. Immediately outside the back door is the sixteenth hole of a golf course, and outside the front door is an old horse trough and the A1 — the old Great North Road. It is a dear little black and cream pub of precisely indeterminate age, perhaps fifteenth or sixteenth century; and Clara, who was born in the bedroom over the public bar, has left the interior exactly as it was in her father and grandfather's day — apart from painting it cream occasion-ally. There are no concessions to ladies in the way of cushions or carpets or anything like that. The bar is contained in a sort of corridor and, in order to drink at it, you have to stand in the line of draught between the front and back doors. On cold evenings everybody, including Clara, abandons the bar and they all go and sit in the tap room where there is a generous fire; anybody who wants a drink goes and gets it.

The pub is full of things that are there because they have always been there: a picture of the waggoner driving along and written beneath him is: 'He who spares the lash can hold the reins more firmly. *Ovid.*' There are old tin trays with a picture of a lady looking like Joan Sutherland, and under her is written: 'She likes it better, it's not bitter.' And there are two Whitbread pale ale men sitting on the mantelpiece and engraved on their pedestals is: 'Good for him, good for you, since seventeen-hundred-and-forty-two.' There are old ginger bottles, and old lemonade bottles with glass stoppers; and the old box Clara uses for something else that says: 'Corry's Slug Death; Taste and They are Dead.' No plastic flowers, no television set, no rubber plants; the hand of time has lain lightly on the Waggoners. 'My customers don't like change,' Clara said. 'Sometimes they say to me, "You've moved that chair." You see, they've known this place as children. You can't really appreciate the atmosphere unless you're a man. It's geared to men, a refuge away from the television and their families.' And she tells the story of how one night the leg came off a table in the public bar, and her customers mended it then and there rather than be without that very table. Even keg, which has swept the country, does not go down well in the Waggoners. 'Not worth the installation,' Clara said.

She is a small, square woman in her fifties, with kind brown eyes and a warmth of manner that combines with a certain dignity to make her remarkable. She went to a convent school and took a secretarial course and thinks she might have gone into the world of commerce. She is clearly an intelligent woman, though they say that to work in a pub that is what you must be. Since 1904, her family have had the Waggoners and since Clara was eighteen, she has devoted her life to it. One wondered how often she got away. She said she came up to London twice a year to go to the dentist.

'Oh, you mean how often do I go away for the *night*?' she said in some surprise. 'I don't suppose I've gone away for the night since before the war.'

She rises at seven and has a cup of tea. Then she cleans the pub, washes the floors, orders the food and sees to the beer for which she has a reputation. She demonstrates and explains about the beer, about tapping the barrel and spiling it. 'Now it will throw off fret,' she said; 'my goodness, this one's lively. Then it will settle down to being placid. I always test it in the morning to see that it's in fine fettle. My customers know their beer, they know if it's one degree off key. I have a chief superintendent comes in here who powerfully enjoys his beer, very critical. You expect to have a nice creamy head on the beer; it improves its appearance enormously and it's nice to have something on your lips that's prickly. So when you pour it, you give it a fair run; you drop it down so there's a splash. The head *ought* to last as long as it takes to drink but of course that depends on the grease of your skin. A woman with lipstick will kill it immediately. It's a menace, that damn lipstick on a glass.'

She is an excellent cook. Talk about the deep freeze — Clara has not even a refrigerator. She produces home-made pies for lunch, hot soup made with real stock, hot bread and the very best Cheddar that she orders from Paxton and Whitfield in Jermyn Street. She makes her own pickles, spices her own vinegar, spreads real beef dripping onto the beef sandwiches and abhors bought horseradish sauce. She has a little herb garden that grows lovage and dill and balm and marjoram. Her only reading, apart from *Golf Illustrated,* is cookery books. She has her customers eating garlic bread and sweet-and-sour red cabbage. The food is delicious for Clara knows how things ought to be done.

The Waggoners was so called because, set on top of the hill, the waggoners taking hay to London would stop to water their horses at the trough outside and themselves with beer inside. Clara can remember the dust of the road and the ditches on either side long before the tar-macadam. After hay wagons came cycling. The cyclists too had to stop at the top of the hill. Then came cars and they did not have to stop. In consequence Clara no longer has much passing trade; she has regulars.

'All walks of life,' she said. 'Everyone from dukes to dustmen. As a matter of fact that's a dustman in the bar now. He helps me with my cellar work.' If you think Clara has a lot to do, she gets by with a little help from her regulars.

Quite often they take over at the bar; they fetch things from the cellar. This is called going down on Safari and the rule is that you whistle all the time you are down there. 'Hello Mr Morris. Would you like to regale yourself with a bottle of Bass? Go down on Safari.' Then the baker came in with long loaves of French bread. 'Freshly caught,' he said, laying them on the counter. 'Oh dear oh *dear*,' laughed Clara. 'Would you like a beer?' The baker said he would have it later. 'Like to put it behind your ear then?' said Clara.

You go through the bar to get to Clara's kitchen which is also her sitting room. There is an open fire with a kettle, always just on the boil, standing on a trivet before it. One sits on the old leather sofa, the clock ticking away, surrounded by all the things that go to make up Clara's life: the ledgers, the cookery books, her sewing basket, her pincushion, her nightie airing in a little niche set in the chimney-breast — and one might be miles away in time and distance. Yet the traffic on the A1 thunders by, a foot from the window.

There came a call for Clara.

'I'm being paged, am I?' she said. It was a lorry driver. 'Can I use your blower, Clara,' he said. 'Oh dear oh dear, are you in trouble?' she said, and suggested that he regale himself with a bottle of beer. Could he use her roller towel? 'I tell you what, Jim,' she said, 'can you fill the coal scuttles in the tap room?'

She likes to play golf; she likes to arrange flowers. She is good at snooker, dominoes, cribbage, and shove ha'penny. She once won a Whitbread cup at darts. She says she is very happy and one believes her. Her life has a calm, a completeness that is enviable. 'I hope I never have to retire,' she said. 'I've had such an enjoyable life, never lonely, never dull. My customers are the nicest bunch you could meet. I'm now serving the grandchildren of people I've known. All with beards and everything and looking like nothing on earth.' Clara laughed indulgently and said this was the life for her.

It is, curiously enough, rarely the older women who complain about their feet or the hard work. Take Lil, for instance, Mrs Lillian Tomlinson. Lil works in the Albion for Mr and Mrs Barnett. She calls Mr Barnett Father, and Mr Barnett wants to know how he can have a daughter older than himself for Lil has a son of thirty-eight. Lil loves work. 'It's not like working at all,' she said. She is the daughter of a policeman, and was nothing more than a respectably married woman when she started helping out in the kitchen of a pub near Oxford Street. But she longed to get at the bar. 'You meet people,' she said. 'You are a bit low in your own life and you can talk to people and it makes the atmosphere so much brighter.'

So she started to work in the bar, and her late husband, who was a lorry-driver, would come and collect her each evening with their three Alsatians. That was twenty years ago and Lil is wonderful at her job. She has a sweet face, soft cheeks with dimples, brown eyes, an extravagantly generous smile and a very round shape. Mr Barnett complains that he is bruised all over by such round ladies behind the bar.

When she is not working, Lil really exists to be teased. She shrieks with laughter and cries out, 'Ooh, isn't he shocking!' 'They torment the life out of me,' Lil said, loving it. The telephone rang and someone said it was for Lil, a person looking for a barmaid who served beer with no knickers on. Lil roared with laughter and said weren't they shocking. Then there were more jokes about her being a female impersonator. And Lil, shaking with laughter, said they tormented the life out of her.

For all the teasing, she is a gentle person. 'You can have a laugh and a joke with it,' she said, 'but once they become serious I don't believe in it. If you are going to listen, you can listen to a lot. But the moment people are on sex I just walk off and wash my glasses. You must keep your glasses — otherwise you're in a muddle. But the ordinary man that comes in here, you might as well say they are the perfect gentleman.' She is the sort of barmaid people tell their troubles to. Indeed she has become so friendly with some of her customers that she has even been to stay with them in Blackpool for her holidays. She has been twice to Canada where her son lives.

One admires her for working and thriving when most women of her age are retiring. 'Nothing to bring on an illness better than moping,' Lil said. She is never ill, her feet are never tired and she never complains about the beer. She was surprised that others did. 'Well,' Lil said, 'they must be very dirty servers to spill beer all over the place. If you serve beer properly you don't spill it. A barmaid should always have her cloth with her when she is serving and she should wipe the bottom of the glass. A barmaid should never be without her cloth.'

When it comes to opening time, Lil puts on a nice frock in readiness. If someone offers her a drink she might have a lager with a dash of lemonade; later she might have a scotch. It is a rule of the house that if they are offered a drink they take it, but if they refuse they don't take the money. She always calls her male customers Sir. 'It's the proper approach,' she said. Opening time drew near. Lil said there was a customer of hers who always came in at three minutes past for a Guinness, and she moved off to get it ready. But she did not make the mistake that a barmaid only makes once — that of assuming that because a man has had a glass of Guinness every night for the past fifty years, that is what he wants tonight. (It is a curiosity of male behaviour that men, the most conservative creatures when it comes to drink, do not like to be thought creatures of habit.) At three minutes past, the man came in.

'What would you like to drink, Sir?' Lil said.

'A Guinness,' said the man.

'A Guinness,' Lil said, as though it were news to her, and fished it out from under the counter.

Very often barmaids marry into the trade, as Mrs Edith Ellaline Clarke will tell you. (What taints the romantic nature of this fact is that licensed victuallers have one of the highest divorce rates in the country — as high as actors though not quite as high as dukes.) But this is not the concern of Mrs Clarke. Her husband is the manager of the Sparrow Hawk in Edgware. Here he and Mrs

Clarke train potential managers, anything up to nine at a time.

Often they marry from the premises. 'Three weddings in September,' Mrs Clarke said, giving the precise dates, 'and now Richard and Jennifer on the twenty-sixth.'

Mrs Clarke is famous for her racy language, her insistence that Godliness comes after cleanliness, and her hopelessly sentimental heart which overflows when people get married and have babies. She has a Robin Hood sense of values, and when they have banquets or weddings in the big dining room, Mrs Clarke is to be found dispensing turkey carcasses and roast potatoes in the public bar.

She is in her late forties, a small plump woman with sharp lively eyes, spectacles and a nice complexion. She is brisk and deft in all her movements and consistent in her attitudes. 'I make sure my swabs are clean; my swabs are boiled every day and my glass cloths the same. I make sure the staff never mix them — otherwise you get flat beer. You teach the staff by driving them, my dear. So we have a little chat. And if their hair is long, I tell them, my dear. I say, "You get your hair cut, my dear."'

She herself rather wanted to be a children's nurse but found herself at the age of fifteen working in her uncle's pub in Chelsea in 1936. She earned 10s. a week, five of which she was made to put in the Post Office. When she was older and the customers offered her a drink, her uncle would say, 'My niece may have a small glass of port.' One day she had one too many and port has never passed her lips since. She usually drinks beer, or if she is tired she will have whisky and ginger. 'Mr Clarke won't start drinking till 9 p.m.' she said.

She is probably the most active woman in England. The Saturday before, with a wedding and other things, she had spent twelve hours on her feet. On the Sunday lunchtime, she was behind the bar again and they had taken £120 in two and a half hours. Often she goes to bed at one; she rises at 8.30. In her leisure, which she maintains she has, she knits patchwork quilts and embroiders pictures, often of dancing couples in national dress, each initialled EEC. The Clarkes, together with the staff, live on the first floor of the pub, a sizeable modern building built more or less in the Tudor style in 1958. Mrs Clarke's snowy white glass cloths danced in the fresh breeze at the back as, together with Mrs Clarke's dog Beauty, we did a tour. One of the girls had failed to make her bed. 'I shall see about *that*,' Mrs Clarke said. 'Come along, Beauty,' and we sailed out. When the couples marry, they move from single rooms to double rooms. Richard and Jennifer were organising such a move.

Mrs Clarke's own sitting room is large and colourful, and packed with gleaming, shining objects: brasses, china clowns, china dogs peeping over the tops of china boots, china ladies with their skirts draped in inviting folds. Lounging in her bedroom were two beautiful cats that they had found wild at the back of the pub. The Clarkes are devoted to animals and to children. Mrs Clarke was lamenting a squirrel they had once had. 'It used to get into bed with us,' she said. 'It used to get into Mr Clarke's pocket.'

She has a month's holiday a year but when she works it is a seven-day week. Occasionally she takes a few hours off to play Bingo. 'I take a few of the girls with me,' she said, 'for Mr Clarke would never come. I sometimes come home with £130.' And then it's drinks all round.

Mrs Clarke adores her life. 'I would recommend it to anybody,' she said. Her heart is warmed by marriages within the trade; indeed, she secretly holds the view that the ordinary young married couple have a very boring time at home on their own in a flat. 'You get bored seeing no one,' she said. 'Sometimes you might feel down in the dumps and then somebody in the bar says something that cheers you up no end.'

Patsy is a well-known (and usually by that name only) part-time barmaid. 'Casual,' she said. 'That's what it's called when you're dodging here and there.' Patsy is a tiny, blonde, middle-aged lady, a fast talker, deliciously scented, with a confiding manner, *very* loud laugh, and a definite air of knowing her way round. She was in a club open to men only, but where Patsy was *persona grata* on account of having so often worked behind the bar. 'We'll have a nice little drink, dear,' Patsy said, bustling through a great many men. Her arrival had not passed unnoticed and they were greeting her in a variety of ways. 'Take no notice, dear,' Patsy said with a wink. And there were many more winks as befitted the nature of the comments. She began to smoke a cigarette in an elegant manner.

She was born in London, south of the river. 'Father was in the print, dear,' she said, 'yes, Father was in the print — hello Joe, hello Reg — come dear, here's your little drink — and so were my two brothers in the print. I started being a barmaid in the theatres really; then I did the races, dear, and the boats, the pleasure steamers from Westminster to Hampton Court which is very interesting, darling, because you see all the pretty little country places. And then the races, Chepstow, Lingfield, Doncaster, Cheltenham, but I got fed up with the travelling. No, I've never been abroad, dear, it hasn't come my way yet, darling. Hello, Bill.'

Bill whispered in her ear.

'*Pardon*,' Patsy said, in French.

PUB

She went on, 'Bill's full of little jokes. I've been told I have a nice personality behind the bar. I always like to be pleasant. Sometimes I wear a little suit, sometimes a little frock and I try to look neat and tidy — hair always nice, nails always nice. And your glasses are as important as the food; must always be clean and polished, and your ash-trays always emptied and keep your eyes open and don't take no bad money and don't forget to pay me twice.' And Patsy collapsed with laughter.

A young man came up and kissed her. 'Hello, mother,' he said.

'You can look but you can't touch,' she cried, delighted. 'He's romancing, of course. I've been divorced so many years now I call myself the little widow. Of course, dear, we never drank when we were young, the same as they do now: vodka and lime, scotch on the rocks, all those soppy little drinks. I suppose I've learnt a lot about men; on the whole they're not bad. Of course I prefer to serve them to women; they're the opposite sex, aren't they? You give them back as good as they give you. If they tell me their stories, I say, "That's stale. I've heard that one before." If they make advances, dear? If they make advances and I like them I play up to them; if not, I do my disappearing act. Leisure, dear? Well, I go round drinking, little clubs in the West End I'm a member of. How many drinks in an evening dear? Well, could be eight or nine. Scotch and water. I'm a very good drinker. I've a good head. Something I've achieved over the years really. No dear, my feet never hurt me and my tongue never hurts me. It's a wonderful life for a barmaid, more so now than ever it was. It keeps you young, all the bending and ducking and diving. Yes, dear, it keeps you young.'

They all say it keeps them young.

PUB

John Fothergill in his book *Confessions of an Innkeeper* says that this is what the barmaid has to do: she has to 'tolerate the bore, encourage the wit, suppress the ass, confess the unburdening, freeze the bottom-pincher, hear the hypochondriacal . . . chairman an argument, eject a drunk, restrain a football team from singing and know where to leave alone the lonely or intrude upon him. She must be a lover of all men; in a philosophic sense, i.e. all women to all men, whether or not she cares, in closing hours, to be one woman to one man.'

And loyal too. The pub is the one place where frailty's name is man, and yet how hard it is to find one barmaid to admit that a customer of hers ever gets drunk. It may well be that some stranger, somebody else's customer gets drunk, but never hers. And how seldom does she refer to the humiliating ritual of drinking-up. Clara has to call out, 'Beddie-bies, beddie-bies', over and over again before she can get her lot to move. One of the Irish girls has to say, 'Let's see you gobble like a turkey.' Jackie Kirkham just calls them darling. 'If you call them darling, it's usually all right,' she said.

Barmaids, more than anyone else, work for the fun of it. 'What I like about this life,' Clara said, 'is a good fire and a good joke.'

'I go down there of an evening,' Mrs Clarke said, 'and I have the old spot of music going. In this life, it's one long party.'

Go to the Inn on any Friday night
And listen to them while they're getting tight
At the expense of him who stands them drinks,
The Mass-Observer with the Hillman Minx.
(Unwitting he of all the knowing winks)
The more he circulates the bitter ales
The longer and the taller grow the tales.
'Ah! this is England,' thinks he, 'rich and pure
As tilth and loam and wains and horse-manure,
Slow — yes. But sociologically sound.'
'Landlord!' he cries, 'the same again all round!'

JOHN BETJEMAN

'The Dear Old Village'
(from *Collected Poems*)

'I don't usually drink this amount, but
I've got my foot trapped.'

✦✦

*Some people hate a pub to change. They love their homely sawdust
floor, spare oh spare that cuspidor. But for some pubs any change
would be a change for the better . . .*

Patrick Campbell

'THEY'VE ABSOLUTELY RUINED IT ...'

His entrance was very good indeed — smooth and practised, the man who knows his local and who is well-
known in it.

He walked straight up to the bar and sat on the third
stool from the left. I guessed that he always used this one,
perhaps because it was opposite the till and he liked,
purely for curiosity's sake, to keep an eye on the takings.

'Usual,' he said to the landlord, 'and the same for my
friend here. How's it going then, Tom?'

'Not bad, squire. The wife's gone up north with the
dogs. Two nice pints.'

I didn't want a nice pint but accepted it rather than
break the flow.

'While the cat's away, eh?'

The landlord chuckled because he had to. 'That it's,
squire. But not a word to Bessie——' If they'd been standing
side by side they'd have nudged one another in the ribs.

'No names, eh Tom, no pack drill?'

'You said it, squire.'

The landlord passed a cloth over the immaculate bar
and moved away.

My friend let him go. Then he cast a derisive eye over
the furnishings of the place. They weren't half bad. Simple
but elegant tables and chairs, a pleasantly unobtrusive
wallpaper and surprisingly attractive tweedy upholstery

on the banquettes around the walls. Even the lighting was agreeable. The brewers had obviously employed some-one with taste, who knew his job.

'They've absolutely ruined it, of course,' my friend said. He lent forward, confidingly. 'I only come here because it's handy. Otherwise I wouldn't touch it with a barge pole.' He drank deeply. 'Absolutely bitched it up,' he said.

I was surprised. His geniality with the landlord was, of course, only a matter of habit but it was strange that he thought the place had been ruined.

'You used to know it before, then?' I said.

Something in my voice caused him to be truthful. 'I never actually came in,' he said, 'but I passed it by many a time. It looked damn cosy from the outside. Just my sort of pub. Not all this modern fiddle-faddle.' He went on, with the confidence of a man who knows he's on a safe wicket, to denounce modern fiddle-faddle in the furnish-ing of public houses. I didn't listen because I had known the pub before. While it did look comparatively cosy, in the old days, from the outside, inside it had been a low-grade sewer.

The first evening I went in there there was a north-east wind howling down the street, carrying with it a good deal of sleet. I was cold and tired after working all day on a television script in a house round the corner and had suddenly thought of a large whisky with ginger wine as an antidote to the horrors of the evening.

I wrenched open the door of the saloon bar, hurrying to get in from the rain, and immediately ran into some-thing that felt and smelled like an unusually heavy shroud. It turned out to be a dank, serge curtain, the colour of old blood, suspended from the ceiling by a thick brass rod.

PUB

After a short struggle I managed to part it, using a finger and a thumb, and walked into the dingiest bar I'd ever seen in my life.

The walls were a dirty yellow, shading into a dark dung colour lower down. The bar itself was short but divided into a number of partitions like loose boxes. The thick glass in these partitions had never been cleaned and were now almost entirely opaque.

The place was lit by three bulbs hanging on long flexes from the ceiling. Two of them had pink paper shades. The other one was bare but it didn't matter because it was out.

At first I thought I was alone in this fearful hole until I saw at the far end of an L-shaped bit — obviously the public bar — the dim figure of an old man bowed over a bottle of brown ale.

He became aware of me at the same time and showed a momentary animation. 'Game a darts, guv?' he said hopefully.

I said I was sorry but I had no time.

'Wanter shaht then,' he said and resumed his silent reverie.

I didn't feel like shouting, nor did I know what to shout, so after a moment I rapped a coin fairly loudly on the counter. Nothing happened. Another curtain the colour of old blood hung in front of what was probably a door leading to the landlord's living quarters but there was no trace of life behind it.

Perhaps a minute went by and then the old man in the public bar raised his head. 'Shop!' he bawled hoarsely. Then he added, equally loudly and hoarsely, 'Nellie!'

'Wanter shaht,' he advised me and fell silent again.

Some time later I became aware of a curious series of noises coming from behind the second curtain. There was also the clump of a stick but it was intermittent, irregular. There was also a spasmodic bumping sound as though a trunk were slithering slowly down the stairs of its own accord. I waiting in some suspense for the curtain to be parted — by I knew not what.

The bumping and clumping came nearer and then stopped. They were supplanted by a low groan. Then the curtain was parted and a large and stately old lady came through it, leaning heavily on a kind of crutch.

At first I thought her whole face was bright, pillar-box red — the symptom, perhaps, of some unspeakable malady — and then I saw that it was rouge, covering the whole of both cheeks.

She said nothing. With some difficulty she lowered herself on to a sawn-off stool behind the bar, settled down and then directed upon me the most unearthly smile I had ever seen. Her lips were painted a kind of purplish red, an altogether different colour to the rouge on her cheeks. Her eyes glittered but without focus. I then saw that the lady was blind drunk. Probably gin, as an antidote to the agonies of arthritis.

I seemed to have been in this nightmare public-house for ever but now there was no drawing back.

'Good evening,' I said. 'May I have a large whisky and some ginger wine? Plain water,' I added, after a moment.

It had no effect upon her of any kind. She continued to sit on the stool. The variegated red face went on beaming at me.

The old man in the public bar decided again to be helpful. 'Screws gotter,' he said, then added in a kindly way, 'pore ole Nell.' Suddenly he shouted 'Fraid!' followed a moment later by 'Shop!' He relapsed once more. He seemed to have made little impression on his glass of brown ale.

PUB

This time fully five minutes appeared to go by before the curtain was agitated again. When it did move it moved almost imperceptibly and then, almost as though he'd walked through it, a little old man with a pale bald head was standing in front of it. He wore two dark waistcoats over a tattered grey cardigan. On his face was a look of surprised apprehension as though he'd been summoned without warning from bed to take charge of a fatal accident.

'Good evening,' I said. 'I'm sorry to disturb you but could I have a large whisky with some ginger — and plain water?'

He looked at me in astonishment for quite a while. His expression now suggested that something outlandish, like an ostrich, had walked into his pub and had started asking, in what might be the English language, for drink.

'Just the whisky would do,' I said, trying to break it up a bit, 'if you haven't got the ginger wine.'

The ostrich, or whatever it was, had spoken again, further deepening the mystery.

He turned his astonished gaze upon poor old Nell but she had no suggestions to offer. He decided upon action. He left me standing in the saloon bar and shuffled slowly into the public. 'Wanta nuvver, Charlie?' he asked the old man.

'Not yet, Fraid,' the old man said. He came to the conclusion that a more elaborate explanation was necessary. 'Aven't finished one wot I got,' he said, pointing to it.

Fraid (Fred?) hung around a bit longer, waiting perhaps for Charlie to finish his drink, but Charlie showed no sign of wishing even to pick it up.

Fraid, baffled and defeated, rearranged some dirty glasses on the counter and then appeared to steel himself for the ordeal.

Looking at the ground, so that perhaps the ostrich-like thing wouldn't come at him too quickly, he came back into the saloon, stood in front of me and suddenly risked all on one single, desperate throw.

'Watcha want, then, guv?' he said, holding on to the bar for support.

'Whisky,' I said. 'And water.'

The scarlet faced old lady suddenly came to life. 'Drop of gin for me, dear,' she said. The long period of silence preceding this request seemed to have done her good. 'Shockin' wevver for the time of year,' she observed, with quite a measure of old-world politeness.

Fraid had poured my drink — a small one — into a very small glass and was about to put it on the counter in front of me when the curtain guarding the street door was flung back so suddenly that the rings actually ran on the corroded brass rail. A short, vital young man stood in the entrance, with his hands on his hips, looking silently round the room with a pair of very, very cold grey eyes. He wore a horsey-looking whipcord suit that was almost champagne coloured and chukka boots of the same shade.

With a certain apprehension I moved out of sight behind one of the partitions. This was a fairly dangerous youth, well known around town at the time.

At the next moment he was in the booth beside me, although I might just as well have been invisible. He greeted Fraid and Nellie with profoundly serious politeness.

'Edwin!' he said. 'And Cecilia! How sweetly pretty you look tonight, my dear.'

I was surprised by the reaction of the two old things. Instead of being terrified, as they should have been, both of them twinkled and simpered as though being called Edwin and Cecilia were the greatest compliment in the world. They murmured inarticulate but delighted little greetings and all at once then the whole saloon bar seemed to be full of rakish and indolent young men. There were a few girls with them but they were drab and dowdy in the extreme.

This, of course, was in the days before Carnaby Street and the mini-skirt, so that the girls were dressed in old mackintoshes and tattered anoraks that had very probably been cast off by their escorts. Their hair was indescribably lank and uncared for and their personalities seemed to be in exactly the same shape.

The men, who were much better dressed, ignored them altogether. With glasses in their hands they leant languidly against the greasy walls of the saloon bar, talking in loud aristocratic voices about hunt balls and polo and house parties in the country. I recognised, having seen their photographs in magazines, a young earl and a couple of lordlets. It was impossible to imagine what they thought they were doing in these revolting surroundings, yet they seemed to be well accustomed to them, almost as though this awful public house was their regular local.

It made me uneasy. Some sort of tribal rite seemed to be taking place, one that was gradually mounting in ecstasy, whatever the nature of the ecstasy might be. Certainly they were becoming more and more polite to Edwin and Cecilia. Even Cecilia — or Nellie, as she had been in the good old days — had so far forgotten her disabilities that she was pouring an occasional drink and trying to deal with the change while Edwin was unmistakably beside himself. The pale little bald head was flushed bright pink as he bustled about behind the bar, saying, 'There's yours, Mr Earl — and that's yours, Sir Lord —'

The young aristocrats received their drinks and these

tributes with grave and perfect courtesy, playing — I became more and more certain — some deadly and derisive game.

One of the young Sir Lords, receiving a drink from Edwin, suddenly stretched out his hand and very delicately, between finger and thumb, felt the edge of the old man's second waistcoat.

'Quite fabulous, Edwin,' he said. 'How did you ever get it so — so — '. He rubbed his finger and thumb together in the air, sensuously, apparently at a loss to describe sufficiently accurately the sensation presented to him by Edwin's waistcoat.

The old man shuffled his feet a bit, delighted that he'd been singled out for this special attention. 'Just an ole weskit, Your Lord,' he mumbled. 'Gotta keep aht the chill, y'know.'

'And to keep it in, too, Edwin,' said the young man gravely.

'That's it, Sir Lord,' said Edwin and chuckled inanely.

It was the most cruel persecution of the poor old thing, I thought, and made all the more cruel by the fact that he didn't even know he was being sent up.

The young man turned his attention to Cecilia who was lowering her fourth or fifth gin since the beginning of the invasion.

'Damme,' he said, 'but I do swear, dear lady, that you grow more handsome by the hour.'

Cecilia goggled at him with her sad red face and the glittering, vacant eye. Then she squirmed a little with pleasure and tried to nudge the young man across the bar. He, however, had withdrawn a little and was clicking an impatient finger.

'Caroline!' he called imperiously, 'my poor drab — come here.'

Caroline slouched up, wearing a dreadfully stained battle-dress jacket, with her thumb hooked into half a tankard of bitter.

'Regard Cecilia,' said the young man tenderly. 'Observe the subtlety of her maquillage. See what that so skilful touch of rouge does to bring up the colour of her eyes. Why cannot you, unhappy slattern, make some similar experiment upon your own unfortunate dial.'

Caroline looked at him briefly. 'Down, Rover!' she said, in the accents of Roedean and moved away.

I'd had enough — enough of the squalor of the place, of the outrageously condescending persecution of poor old Nellie and Fred and most of all of the feeling that something horrible was going on that I didn't understand. I began to sidle out of my corner of the booth when something happened so quickly that for a moment I didn't take it in.

The curtain leading to the street had been pulled back. A young man stood there wearing round metal-rimmed glasses and a neat blue suit. I think he even had a grey trilby hat. But suddenly the glasses and the hat were obliterated by a cascade of beer that struck him full in the face. For a second it seemed that the beer had simply come out of the air and then I saw that the tankard in the hand of the fairly dangerous young man in the whipcord suit was empty, when it had been full a moment before. Scarcely without turning round he had flung a whole pint of beer clean across the room, to catch the new arrival right between the eyes. The unfortunate young man disappeared, without saying a single word, back into the night.

The one in the whipcord suit looked at me with his expressionless cold grey eye. 'Dreadful little chap,' he said levelly, though I could see that he was breathing quickly, excited by the action. 'That wretched, smooth suit,' he said. 'And the hat is *new.*' There was an extra-ordinary malevolence behind this innocent word. 'You see,' he said to me and then paused, looking for the right name, 'you see — Marmaduke — we're texture men. That's why we come here. We like it greasy, thick, nubbly, unwholesome — like the unspeakable cardigan worn by the loathsome little landlord, like, indeed, Caroline's fabulously fusty battledress. Now, Marmaduke,' he said, 'is there anything I can do for you . . .?'

'Not at the moment, thank you,' I said. I happened to be wearing a suit fairly smooth to the touch. 'Goodbye,' I said and made for the door. As I left I seemed to hear a faint voice from far away. 'Game a darts, guv?' It was the old man in the public bar, quite unmoved by all that had gone before.

Outside the sleet had turned to hail. It felt delightful on my face.

'Well, as the man said, a bird never flew on one wing. Let's have the same again, Tom. My friend here will pay.'

I found I was still sitting in this charming little pub, with the tasteful furnishings and the tweedy up-holstery on the banquettes around the walls. It was impossible to imagine that it was the same place in which poor Edwin and Cecilia had been tormented, in which the old man had waited for ever for a game of darts and in which the unfortunate new arrival had had beer flung in his face because he was wearing a new hat.

'Absolutely ruined,' my friend said, probably for the tenth time, but now having reached a conclusion.

'Not absolutely,' I said. 'I rather like that nubbly upholstery. You see,' I told him, 'myself, I'm a kind of texture man.'

There's no mistaking a Welsh pub. From the outside it may look like an English pub, a Scottish pub, an Irish pub. But inside, it's full of Welshmen . . .

Gwyn Thomas

SOME INNS IN WALES

Wales is a small enough country: it can be worn like a garment. Its taverns, running its length and breadth like golden buttons, hold it in place. At the thought of them the echoes of songs richly harmonised move about my mind, fragments of astonishing conversations, hushed abruptly by the knife of licensed hours, glint through one's memory.

This roll-call will have to be infuriatingly partial. Most men have special pubs whose sight and sound colour the core of their entire civilisation. There will be many whose favourite resting-places will have, willy-nilly, to be omitted from this recollection, and they may well take offence. To them I sorrowfully apologise.

So much depends on the length of one's tether, the hour of one's passage through a particular town. I salute all the snugs and bar-parlours I have never had the privilege to know, and the men whose evenings they have enriched.

PUB

It is a good experience to go the rounds of a group of familiar pubs with a stranger. When you are interpreting an old and deeply loved phenomenon to one coming in from the outside, your eyes work overtime. Details of delight to which one had grown too used dance back with fresh vitality into the centre of one's senses.

Some years ago I had that sort of luck. I was visited by the American writer Jay Williams. Jay loves Britain. When he wrote his first novel he did not take as his theme the crackling, violent New York of the 1930s where he grew up. The tale he told was of Robin Hood and Sherwood Forest. His mind had written its own exit-visa to a simpler time and place. He was obsessed by the twanging fluency of insurgent bowmen and the thought of roadside taverns and forest beer-houses shaking and bulging with the laughter of rebels and bandits celebrating their latest deliverance from the sheriff and the noose.

I took him to his first Welsh pub. It was a genial house called the Park Hotel in Barry, Glamorgan. It had been my local for years. Each Saturday night I had been one of a modest choral group who swung into action, moved by a lyrical tide, around half-past nine. Our best item was 'Good Night, Ladies', sung very softly. It had taken a long time to master this pianissimo effect because the Welsh larynx is a noisy article and prone to bawl.

Next to 'Good Night, Ladies' was 'Wrap Me Up In My Tarpaulin Jacket', sung at normal volume and with a lot of emotional force. One of our number was an old and sentimental captain of the Merchant Marine. When we got to the end of 'Tarpaulin Jacket' he would burst into the bitterest tears, his mind flooded by memories of sea-going friends who would never again come ashore. He would instantly repent of his weakness. (His reputation at sea had been that of a sulphurous tyrant ready at the drop of an oath to fell any potential mutineer with fist or marlinspike.)

To make amends for his display of emotion he would order two complete rounds for the whole roomful of us. Never was a gesture so loudly applauded and never was 'Tarpaulin Jacket' flung back into the programme so often by needy choristers who regarded the old captain as the next best thing to direct Government aid.

It was to this snug that I introduced Jay. He was not impressed by the music. All British songs, he said, sounded the same to his ear and even the old captain, venting his grief, he regarded as a subtle kind of Welsh comedian. When he heard 'Tarpaulin Jacket' he said, politely, that it was the best rendering of 'All Through The Night' he had ever heard.

But when I went to the bar and ordered two Nut Brown Ales, a famous local bottled beer, his eyes glinted with excitement. This was the true idiom of Sherwood and the Nottingham boyos. He looked for all the world as if he expected the ale to be delivered by arrow, and he gazed at the elderly and rather dour lady behind the bar as if she were the very sister of Maid Marian.

The last but one item of those Saturday musical sessions was a solo from the landlord, Bill Morse. He only knew one song, 'I Have Heard The Mavis Singing', and never has the mavis sung on a more uneven wicket. Bill was as worthy and kind a man as ever breathed on this earth. He had served, during his apprentice years, as a potman in some of the roughest pubs in Cardiff's dockland. Time and prosperity had tempered and softened him.

When he sang 'The Mavis' he seemed to be trying to restore some innocence shattered during the turbulent years of his early manhood and we sympathised with his

mood. But his style of singing was so vague and tremu-
lous you could hear every mavis in the world moulting
with worry. Even Bill's Sealyham dog, normally an
animal too blithe for comfort, came into the snug, lay
down and gave out with low, complaining howls which
were a clear improvement on Bill. We reacted in the same
way as the Sealyham but we heard him out in grave,
silent courtesy. Bill always showed his gratitude by buying us a round. Between Bill and the old captain we did
fine.

Jay listened carefully to Bill and said that Bill's vocal
style and that particular song, combined, must have
caused the methane that hastened Britain's decline as a
world power.

Jay was eager to dip into the magic well of friendship,
tolerance and laughter that nourishes the culture of our
pub life. When I told him that on fine days I often did a
six-mile circular walk through the lanes of the adjacent
countryside, calling in at selected inns to relieve thirst and
silence, he said he would join me at the first opportunity.

There is a good cluster of pubs in that eastern part of
the Vale of Glamorgan, paced out perfectly to suit the
needs of a rambler. Our first call was at the Three
Horseshoes in Moulton. Until fifteen years ago it was a
very old-fashioned house indeed, kept by an ancient
couple with a taste for shadow. The vital business of the
place was conducted in one small room flanked by
benches of a low, penitential sort. Transactions were
carried on in low voices and the air of mystery never
lifted. With a few peep-holes in the door it would have
been a dead-ringer for the more tight-lipped sort of
speakeasy.

When the old people retired the Horseshoes was

dragged into the modern age by a brilliant and resource-ful landlord. Rooms that seemed to have been sealed off for centuries were opened, sharply furnished and superbly lit. Food sizzled and moved from oven to table at a speed that left customers, who had known the old regime, shaking their heads with shock and ducking with alarm.

Chicken in the Mitt reached its British apogee. Roasted poultry flew like shrapnel. If one, in conversation, over-gesticulated with one particular hand one found a chicken in it. This provided a good way of emphasising certain points.

In the early days the waitresses were over-literal. One day I was staring at my chicken and chips. There was no cutlery. I called to the barmaid, 'What about some tools to go along with this, Olive?' 'It's not allowed,' said Olive. 'The cutlery isn't allowed, Mr Thomas. It's in the mitt, in the mitt.' And she did a quick impression of Tarzan tearing his prey with his bare hands and wiping his hands on his fur bikini. I had to point out to her that I was wearing cloth and had not directly handled a chip since my Rhondda childhood. A sweet place.

Our next call was at the Fox and Hounds in Llancarfan. The village lies in an enchanting dingle and stands up to its top-hair in historical memory. It once formed part of the great but now utterly vanished university of Llan-twit Major. Its dominion began to falter when bands of raiding Vikings fell upon it and struck heavy blows for illiteracy. Six Celtic princes were once in residence there as students, and this fact is often dredged up by people who feel that the centuries have provided too drastic a declension of academic dignity in the area and who are agitating for a larger chalk grant for the local primary schools.

PUB

Not long ago excavations took place in Llancarfan to clear a site for new building. A skeleton was found in a standing posture. At first it was thought to be that of a dawdling hodman who had failed to keep up with his mason, but it was announced later that it was that of a monk who had been walled up for some misdemeanour or other. It was noted that the skeleton had its right arm pointing at the door of the Fox and Hounds as if in mute bequest.

Between our two half-pints Jay and I had a look at the Norman Church, a squat, strong structure that still looks as if it has one eye cocked for Viking looters who might come trampling down the road from the coast. On the floor of the aisle we saw a curious thing: seven dead bats arranged nearly in a straight line. We assumed that they were victims of some skilled fumigator who had been briefed to expel the death-watch beetle which was at the time active among the rafters. But there was something about the position of the cadavers, some hint of ritual, that worried Jay. He found the sexton, a scholarly man. 'What's with the seven dead bats in the aisle?' 'Heretics,' said the sexton, and we had to take his word for it.

We continued our walk to Llancadle and the Green Dragon. During the years after the last war old Tom Evans held court there in the manner of Dr Johnson, sitting in the ingle, winter and summer, always convinced that the weather outside was doing its arctic worst. His drink was whisky and hot water, heavily sugared and he had a huge brass kettle at his elbow, perpetually on the boil and giving out steam on a scale to power every train in Wales and parboil most of Tom's friends.

After his fourth hot toddy he would break the current of his talk on philosophic and antiquarian matters which he loved and stare in turns with a most perplexed look at the circle of his cronies. Either he would advance some new thesis about the walled-up monk in Llancarfan and the nature of the offence that had made his abbot so vindictive, or he would say, 'You know Burton Hill?'

We all knew Burton Hill. It was a fantastically bent and steep ascent on the main road nearby, dangerous as bubonic since the coming of the car. The ground at the foot of this hill was subject to frequent and severe flooding.

'You remember Hughes the Milkman?' asked Tom.

Few of us remembered Hughes but he had become familiar to us through Tom's regular evocations. 'Hughes delivered his last pint in one of the wettest Januaries known in this parish, and this parish was once called, for the power of its monsoons, the urinal of the earth. Hughes was depressed that morning and he laced himself with a few brandies before setting forth with his horse and cart and his two big churns. He must have given his horse a tot or two as well for the horse, that morning, was seen to gallop. Hughes went down Burton Hill like a charioteer. The water had come up that night and had flooded the little valley to a great depth. Hughes went right into it. Never seen again. Hughes, the horse, the churns, never seen again. There were some who said it was divine vengeance because Hughes had been watering his milk so intensely for thirty-one years his cows could be seen poking their heads over the hedge and trying to explain. That walled-up monk in Llancarfan and Hughes, they are out there somewhere now, discussing their dilemma.'

At the crossroads not far from the Green Dragon we took the bus to Llantwit Major. We passed near Gileston railway station used during the war by the horde of airmen serving at neighbouring St Athan's. The Gileston station was said to have rivalled Bombay in the number of phoney railway tickets palmed off on harassed collectors in poor light.

Llantwit Major is a town of inscrutable antiquity. Dr Glyn Daniel, in his earliest phase as an archaeologist, uncovered a tessellated Roman pavement beneath a local bakery. The news touched some deep nerve of civic pride and no one since has been able to nibble at a loaf without hearing the bugles of the legions blow.

At one time Llantwit was little more than a vast cluster of pubs. Which might be a clue to the age and decline of the place. Such an aggregation of inns would have served a city and as the city and its colleges shrank, more and more places of revelry and light sank into disuse, silence and darkness. This provided a field-day for the militant puritans whose restrictive phobias chiselled the heart out of Wales. In Llantwit, still a very Welsh place, the sound of the harp was replaced by the twang of licences being revoked and tavern doors clanged shut. When the joyful place fell below a certain number even the Vikings, on their annual rounds of looting, stopped calling.

But there is still a fair selection. On the square three pubs stand in handsome proximity: the White Hart, the Globe and the Swan. If they were any closer they would embarrass each other's barrels. They share the square with a chip-shop which, in moods of Saturday night abandon, becomes a commercial hinge of the region.

Of the three pubs the Swan is the most picturesque. It has walls as thick as Hadrian's anti-Pict barrier and a fine collection of subtly shaped settles in the public bar. In that same bar is a photograph of Lloyd George receiving the freedom of Cowbridge, the acclaim of its burgesses and looking as if there was nothing surprising in this.

The Swan has a special place in the mythology of this area. Quite apart from serving beer which has a marvellous tingle about it, as if drawn from a deep and frosted well, and the suggestion given by its walls and slit windows of having been a fortress since the beginning of time and hostility, it played a large part in the local saga of the American press millionaire and versatile megalomaniac, William Randolph Hearst. If his newspapers ran short of wars to report, Hearst would tell the State Department to buck up its ideas and start one.

He also went around Europe, buying historic buildings and shipping them to America. It is said that he bought an Italian abbey and set it down in California with three monks still clinging defiantly to it and kicking up a great fuss until Hearst, a man not normally patient with the clergy, relented and included them in the contract.

He bought St Donat's castle, two or three miles from Llantwit Major and used it as a regal frame for himself and his friend, the film actress, Marion Davies. In its long cycles of peace and brigandage, penury and success, St Donat's castle must have known some peculiar assemblies of people, but none more bizarre than those convened by W. R. Hearst. He invited as resident guests a unique turnout of top performers from Hollywood, then in its lushest epoch, the Twenties and Thirties. Drifts of starlight fell on the time-grey township.

The guests fell in love with Llantwit and especially, for its great age and quaintness, with the Swan. In their sports cars they roared to its doors through the town's tiny and perilous streets, the biggest thing in sensational noise since two rival male voice parties, inflamed by a malicious adjudication, had surged around the walls of the Guildhall, over the road from the Swan, beating the senses out of each other to the precise rhythm of the song they had just sung competitively in the eisteddfod marquee.

PUB

On the day that Jay Williams and I called in, the fire was large, the beer supreme and the air ripe for talk. We got into conversation with an old man. As far as we could make out, for his style was jerky and conspiratorial, he was a hedger who was making no great effort to keep in continuous touch with hedges. The scandals and delights of the Hearst occupation were still loud on his tongue. Tales of Babylonian excess, he told us, had spread like Welsh rain, and he had kept his ear close to Llantwit's quaking ground, a faithful recorder of every new shock. 'I've seen them all come filing through that door. The screen's reigning monarchs. Clark Gable, he's been as near to me as I am to you now. Gary Cooper, the lean plainsman, I've touched him. No airs, no side. Up with the glass. Down with the ale. And always an inquiry about the rheumatism in my legs. Rheumatism is the curse of hedging, my trade. Constance Bennett sat on that very settle you're on at this moment. There was beauty. Her perfume was rare, too potent for a hedger who lives in a world of simpler smells.'

The old man's grasp on truth was shaky. He mentioned many actresses as having been among Hearst's guests who could not possibly have been so. He was riding a tide of elegy that made him eager to include the whole of theatrical humanity inside the walls of the Swan. We asked him if Nell Gwynn had ever been among the number.

'Oh, often, often. Here every whipstitch, Nell.'

He had briefly been employed at the castle during Hearst's Glamorgan heyday. He had a story of having been at the top of a tall ladder, cleaning a window or lopping ivy. His voice shook when he told this story and he was hard to follow. At the window appeared a female face. It was Elinor Glyn, the romantic novelist and a woman who cared for her beauty. Her face that morning was covered with a thick mud pack and her eyes, as far as they could be seen, were glinting with rage at the hedger's intrusion. She looked like an excited gargoyle, and in his astonishment the hedger did about the only reasonable thing. He fell off the ladder. 'But some of the lady guests fancied me. Had thousands of pints with them in this very room. Never paid a penny. Bit of a favourite with them, I was. One of them came after me in the woods one day, the woods that run down to the edge of the sea. She was shouting, 'I want to know about Welsh peasants. I've heard a lot about Welsh peasants. Come back here, Welsh peasant!' Of course, I legged it. Wouldn't have been proper, not with me taking wages off Mr Hearst.'

He looked wistfully around the room.

'Mr Hearst, Mr Gable, Mr Cooper, all gone. All gentleman.' He pointed at the picture of Lloyd George receiving the freedom of Cowbridge. 'Not like him. Not reliable that one. When he was visiting Mr Hearst, he was in his car and I was hedging. He swerved to avoid something. Caught me with a bumper and I went clean through the hedge. And I was half-way through a swinging movement with a billhook. Try that sometime. Tricky. Always swerving, that Lloyd George.'

Mr Hearst, Mr Gable, Mr Cooper, all gone. But the Swan, the White Hart, the Globe, still stand four-square against time, everlastingly warm and welcoming.

On the way back to Barry we called at the Blue Anchor. It must be the oldest inn still standing in Glamorgan. Jay was delighted to realise that when the Blue Anchor's walls were going up, Robin Hood was just about drawing a bead on his first Nottingham constable. Its original walls were of a size to constitute a world in themselves. One of the existing rooms was hewn out of solid stonework.

The legend is that an intricate system of tunnels once led from the pub to the sea's edge and provided a busy hub for the local smuggling traffic.

The legend is resonant and moving after centuries of puritanism and the pox of taxation for taxation's sake. One can imagine the dedicated anti-revenue delinquents shuffling along their tunnels, surfacing through the flagstones of the Anchor singing whatever anthem they used to celebrate the imminent drenching of the zone in duty-free brandy. Today, after every increase in taxes on beer and spirits, customers are seen jumping heavily on the ground around the Anchor, trying to find if any of those tunnels are still viable.

On the bus home, Jay and I talked of the British folk who had crossed the Atlantic in their little ships to fill and fertilise the American wilderness. 'Ships, my foot,' he said. 'They were taken on the sort of tour you've treated me to today and they just floated over to New England.'

There is a line of territory in South Wales which is not likely to become an international tourist trip. But, with its attendant pubs, it could be a great tonic for both eye and spirit. It stretches from the countryside north of Cardiff to the top of the Rhondda Valley, once the heart of our coal industry, now with one colliery left, gaping in absolute astonishment at the antics of the fuel-power game.

The first lap of our journey is a triangle of villages with remarkable names: Creigiau, Castellau, Beddau. Craggs, Castles, Graves. A fine, sombre summary of mediaeval violence. Castellau was the scene in my early days of a great annual festival of singing. As a boy alto I jugged up on lemonade outside the Lamb and Flag while our elders, inside, prepared for some of the most intense choral contests of the period.

PUB

At Creigiau we have the Caesar's Arms, transformed from ancient dereliction by Billy and Glen, two of the region's most imaginative victuallers, who once waved a similar wand of magic over the White Hart at Llantwit. My older brothers and sisters who often walked from the Rhondda to Creigiau remember the Caesar's Arms when its landlord was a blind harpist who played softly to the customers when the beer was perfect and loudly when it was slightly off.

Nearby is Llantrisant on its hill which, give or take a priest or bull or two, is a twin of Toledo in Spain. Llantrisant was the home of Dr William Price who went through life leaving a wake of notable oddities behind him. He named his son Jesus Christ the Second and pioneered cremation. For both these acts he was nearly lynched and owed his survival to a few alert gendarmes and personal footwork as alert as Jimmy Wilde's.

Also in Llantrisant is the Butcher's Arms, a gracious house whose lady in command is Miss Winnie Dancer. You will hear her name in any conversation about the licensed trade in south-east Wales. For her, Llantrisant is a harbour of quietness. She came here from the Volunteer, a clamorous tavern in the middle of Cardiff and the Maltsters, one of Llandaff's close-knit group of cosy taverns within bell-shot of the cathedral.

Winnie has a green and somnolent parrot called Verdant. The bird is upset only by customers who don't get its name quite right and call it Vernon or even Verdun. Verdant was once employed as an extra in a television play. For this occasion it worked out a new line of dialogue. Throughout the session it kept saying, 'Quiet, quiet!' This had a great effect on technicians and performers and ensured a uniquely jerky production.

Just to the north of Llantrisant is the great rocky ridge

that separates the Vale of Glamorgan from the Rhondda Valley. At Trebanog, the first village to give you a view of the huge splits that make the Big and Little Rhonddas, we have the Black Diamond, the only pub I ever recall as having a fives court, never to my knowledge played on.

Down the hill towards Porth is my native village, Cymmer. The Cymmer Hotel, solid and sedately Victorian, still stands opposite the old churchyard, beyond which are the remains of one of the biggest collieries in Britain. The graveyard has been mutilated by violent subsidence and must contain the most disturbed group of dead people since the invention of mortality. At the foot of the graveyard once stood the New Inn. Early in its life the New Inn began to quake as the top soil shook and lapsed. Custom fell away until every male voice singing group turned up to give support. They turned up on the same night and sang with a passion not heard before. It was too much for the New Inn's parlous fabric. The roof caved in, scattering the vocalists like chaff.

On the corner that formally divides the valley in two is the Tynewydd Hotel. In one of its smaller lounges is an unforgettable photograph. It shows the survivors of the disaster that flooded, in 1870, a pit that occupied the present site of the Tynewydd. More sensitive customers say that on quiet nights, between sips, they can hear the floodwaters far below glugging and sucking ground in the dark. I've listened. I've heard nothing. Gulps of noisy relish from my companions, but no flood waters. The Welsh are utterly neurotic about water.

The Rhondda has many and fascinating pubs, bastions of sanity in the face of a social and industrial set-up that always struck me as more than slightly out of plumb. One I will always recall with affection is the Pengelly in Treorchy. In the back room there, one could hear members of the Treorchy Male Voice Choir experimenting between walls that provided a pampering acoustic, with new harmonies after the rigours of a formal rehearsal. And, during each pause in the singing, pub-talk of the most brightly uproarious kind.

But leaping out of the peopled and familiar part of Wales, what pub speaks most loudly to the mind? I would say the Crossed Foxes, a few miles to the south of Dolgellau. Once, on my way to the Crossed Foxes, I walked up the Dinas Mawddwy pass, a back-breaking slope. The hour was later than I had bargained for and each slow step I took seemed to thicken the shadows. In that part of Wales, even when you are not walking through a haunted dusk, the air can start vibrating with immemorial echoes and history can fall in at your side. It did with me that night.

The hillsides stirred with the ghosts of Glyndwr's men moving east to break teeth and hearts against the hard judgments of time, ability and power. And among the phantom convention were the Red-Haired Bandits of Dinas Mawddwy who once infested that area. They were an enterprising and ruthless bunch who had a way, when rebuffed at the front door, of coming down the chimney to sack innumerable households. When society got them in its sights at last so many of them were left dangling on so many trees even now the Forestry Commission throws a little salt over its shoulder before earthing the next sapling.

By the time I reached the lip of the pass, darkness was utter and my nerves in a rare old state. One part of my mind was applying for a spear in the hosts of Glyndwr. The other part was whimpering to do a deal with the Normans. Then before me and clear as all the stars combined were the golden windows of the Crossed

Foxes, the only lights to be seen on earth in that particular place.

And within twenty minutes I was talking, eating, drinking, laughing with full delight. If I never attain a higher ecstasy than that I will not complain.

❈

Now the labourers look well resting in their white shirts at the doors of rural ale-houses. Now an elm is fine there, with a seat under it; and horses drink out of the trough, stretching their yearning necks with loosened collars; and the traveller calls for his glass of ale, having been without one for more than ten minutes; and his horse stands wincing at the flies, giving sharp shivers of his skin, and moving to and fro his ineffectual docked tail; and now Miss Betty Wilson, the host's daughter, comes streaming forth in a flowered gown and ear-rings, carrying with four of her beautiful fingers the foaming glass, for which, after the traveller has drank it, she receives with an indifferent eye, looking another way, the lawful twopence.

LEIGH HUNT

'I need a drink!'

✿✿

Some people seem to live in a pub.
Others really do live in a pub.
Miss Nancy Banks-Smith managed to be brought up in a pub.
It gives her a certain cachet in serious drinking circles.

Nancy Banks-Smith

THE PUB THAT WE CALLED HOME

Everyone called it New Pub except my mother who called it an hotel, taking pains with the unaccustomed aitch. It must have been new in 1901 because that was the date carved in stone high on the wall, higher than the surrounding chimney pots.

Built like a palace or a prison. A great white-stoned step flanked with brawn-coloured columns and my father's name in gilt above that. And up to a balcony with a flagpole and up to the great green dome that had once been gold.

It had been surrounded by mill chimneys, straight as sentinels but they had mostly come down. A mill chimney falls slow and stiff at first then breaks its back and comes down with a crumbling thunder. The valley was depressed. You might say skint — but depressed is right too. It looked as if God's bottom had sat on the place, making the terraced houses squat and the people short. Even their caps looked as if they had been sat on.

Most people coming to London feel small. But I actually was small. I didn't know till I left the valley that women grew that tall and flawless. No one was short or distorted or florid or pallid or carried that unmistakable physical stamp Made in Lancashire.

My grandmother said it came from standing at a loom. 'Your great-aunt Selina was bandy from working seven looms at seven. She was so little they had to stand her on a box.' And the men said there was never a footballer like Little Jimmy who got the ball by diving through the legs of the chap as had it. But I'd say it was malnutrition. Go short and you grow short. Food was always bought cooked, perhaps because all the women worked. There was work for women when there was none for men. Meat pudding with-or-without-gravy and bring-your-own-basin from the baker. Fish and chips and tripe and vinegar. Pork pies and potato pies. We sold those. They came on wooden trays so wide I couldn't grasp both handles and when they were sold they left greasy ghosts, shining circles on the paper where they had been. And when there was a darts match we made hot-pot in a basin as big as a sink.

Massive, immovable and marble-halled, the pub was built as if Victoria would always be queen and cotton her consort. There was a fat statue of her where the buses stopped and the streets were called after her, her children and her jubilee. But even the knocker-up, who tapped on first floor windows with a long pole in the dark dawn, was out of work because the weavers were.

The pubs and pawnbrokers were still in business. My parents took the pub because they owned a baker's shop and people stopped buying cake. They weren't buying two loaves either where one would do and every evening my father took the van round the streets trying to sell the last of the bread. But Christmas was the crunch. Every shelf was snowy with Christmas cakes but the big shop across the road was giving away Christmas cakes with every order. 'They were no bigger than this,' said my mother curving her hands to the diameter of a tea-cup, but they were free. We sold one to a friend who called and found my mother crying among the spectacular stock, all ribboned and flower-crowned like white brides left at the altar.

They took the pub in the new year.

I was five and hadn't lived with my parents much. The day I was born my father scattered cake crumbs round the shop shouting, 'Let's give the mice a treat', but it was also the first year of the slump. As they worked harder, they had less time for me. I lived with grandparents off and on and the day I arrived to live at the pub they had a toy waiting for me like butter for the paws of a new kitten.

It was part of the pub's inventory. A cast-iron nigger minstrel as big as myself with a wide, smiling mouth. You gave him a penny and he swallowed it. They stood around and gave me pennies, watching me work it and wondering if I'd settle. I was subdued by such close attention and wanted to say that what I really liked were the thick curtains on big, brass, rattling rings that hung over every door to keep out draughts.

It must have been cold because there were fires in every room and when it was open men stood and steamed and when it wasn't maidens draped with inverted knickers steamed round the fire instead. Maidens? You call them clothes-horses. Perhaps it was a joke as a maiden is a horse that hasn't won a race. They were dedicated gambling men, the customers. They kept fighting cocks, raced pigeons and whippets and were bookies' runners. I never saw anyone in the public bar read anything but the back page of the paper. It carried the day's racing.

Maybe it was less cold than damp. A little river looped around the pub and overflowed every winter into the cellar lifting the barrels and boxes and bottles. When it went down marooned frogs croaked from cold stone corners in the shipwrecked cellar.

You wore clogs on weekdays not because they were

cheap, because they weren't. But they were warm and waterproof and when the iron wore thin the clogger reshod them like a horse. If your feet did get soaked you put them in a mustard bath — just a bucket with mustard and hot water. And if you had a cold on your chest you applied a mustard plaster. Or rather got someone else to apply it. For mustard plasters burned and the first (and second and third) reaction was to tear it off. Billy, a brickie by day and a waiter by night, was impervious to the pleas of the patient. Every winter arose the shriek 'Tek it off' and Billy's reply, 'Not fer a brass clock'.

We had those too. Brass clocks. They had pillars and ladies wearing roller towels and a little roof over the lot. To keep off the rain, I supposed.

It was considered soft to complain about illness. And, possibly, it was inadvisable. For the home-grown remedies the cook and cellarman, the cleaners and waiters, swallowed to keep the damp out of their bones were worse than the complaint. My grandmother's dandelion and burdock was highly thought of for rheumatism (I gathered the ingredients in the garden) and I cannot possibly convey the memorable awfulness of her brimstone and treacle. I have found in her nostrum book a 'sure cure for the first stage of consumption' involving unshelled eggs, lemon juice and sugar candy left till mouldy then beaten up in a pint of white rum. On the next page is a specimen letter of condolence to the bereaved: 'Perhaps, when we all meet in the Great Beyond, we shall understand . . .' I can hear a brewer's drayman shouting aloud as my father poured iodine into his gashed arm. A pub was expected to provide rough and ready first aid.

No one, in my memory, ever had an illness, they 'just missed' something worse. The time I 'just missed' meningitis (I still don't know what I actually had) there was no one in the pub but Convict 99. With a fine disregard for people who had paid their debt to society, everyone called him Ninety-nine. Nobody knew what he had done, as nobody knew what the V.C. had done who sat antique and waiting to be treated in the corner by the door. Or even which war he had done it in.

Ninety-nine, who looked formidable even in a bar where all wore buckled belts and some were reputed to use them, was despatched to fetch the doctor. He ran all the way and, without stopping, into the surgery where the doctor was applying his stethescope to the first chest of the day. 'Kid at pub's poorly.' The doctor said he would be down when surgery was over and kindly close the door behind you.

'Get thi bag and shut thi gob,' said Ninety-nine with classic conciseness. The doctor arrived immediately and had to be revived with brandy. Ninety-Nine returned a little later, having forgotten to sup up his pint.

The rougher the diamond the kinder they were to me. They gave me wrapped toffees from their pockets and told me to mind me sums. I took the toffees but not, I regret, the advice.

It's coming out sad. But it shouldn't, for though the time was sombre, the pub was the place they came to be happy. And they were. On the most unpromising occasions. Weddings were good for business but funerals were better for they had the insurance money. Women in the snuff box, who normally brought a milk jug, came with the big, pot-bellied water jug from the wash stand for a funeral.

The snuff box was for old women only as the vault was for men. 'Is oo theer?' a husband, momentarily mindful of his missus, would ask. And oo usually was. It was only at university that I learned that oo is in the purest line of descent from *heo*, the Anglo-Saxon feminine. It was the language of Beowulf.

The kitchen was for men only too. But a cut above the vault. They wore braces and had a picture of Napoleon on board the *Bellerophon* and paid twopence extra to have their drinks brought on a tray. I still carry a tray with my fingers *so*, the hand like a spider on its back. That way you can raise it high above a crowd, swing it low to a table and still have a hand free to pick up glasses as you go.

The billiard room was for 'a better class of person altogether'. It was usually empty.

If a man actually wanted to drink with his wife he wore a trilby and went into the bar parlour. Or the commercial room at weekends where the girls took their hair out of curlers which they had worn all week and everyone came early to get a good seat for the sing-song. I went to sleep for years to the warm roar of 'There's An Old Mill By the Stream, Nellie Dean'. And, as I stayed up later, to 'Good old pals, Jolly old pals' and 'Roll me over, I'm in clover', the last songs of the night. And to 'Time, gentlemen, please.'

The warm roar was safe and normal. The harsh-sweet solos, the shouted orders, the clamour of bells. Silence was danger — a police raid. George Dixon was still Jack Warner then, minding his bike and his own business and we hadn't learned to love the law. My parents went white and polite at the sight of a uniform for if they lost their licence they lost both home and job instantaneously. The police were after betting slips and never, surprisingly, found them in the big, blue china aspidistra pots. If the aspidistra was dry no harm was done. If it had been watered the slips were fished out, soggy and indecipherable.

PUB

We kept an assortment of Alsatians, Sam and the sons of Sam, and when a policeman found the front door ajar one afternoon and came in to investigate he was pinned in a corner by Sam himself, whose temper had not improved with age. The policeman's own temper had deteriorated when my parents returned from the afternoon drive, which was the only break they could ever take together. But it was generally agreed among the bookies' runners that Sam's arrest had gloriously crowned his long and loyal life. Dogs were expected to earn their keep. Good ratters and racing whippets shivered under the benches in the vault.

I was fond of animals because I had few friends. Mainly because of my mother's order not to run about the streets like nobody's child. I didn't know which I envied more: the children who tobogganed black and happy down tips on tin trays or the Queen of the May, her hair ringleted from a night in rag curlers, who came round with the maypole dancers. They were children, like carollers, and they knew as everyone did that a pub was an easy touch.

So I played like a princess or prisoner inside the eight foot wall which ran around our bowling green and empty stables and great cobbled courtyard. The bowling green was once smooth velvet and heaved in the middle as if it was breathing. But it ran wild, perhaps during the war or perhaps because if you are bowling you aren't boozing and that is bad for business. The animals lived in and on the long grass. They ate and, in time, were eaten. The milkman's knackered pony which sometimes, daring, I rode around the streets to urchin suggestions that I should 'Gerrof and milk it'. The hens which were raffled at Christmas and the rabbits which always got out and ran as if their lives depended on it. Which they did.

And the nanny goat. I loved that goat because I thought that goat loved me from the way it nibbled my clothes and fingers. It ate the crown of a customer's billycock once and would have eaten the brim if it hadn't lodged round its neck like a halter.

But it caught pneumonia and died. My father poured the best brandy down its throat till its square, satanic eyes glazed. He said it died happy.

He was the sunniest, funniest and most sociable man I ever knew. He could, as the pub put it, talk the hind leg off a donkey. Sketchily educated, I suppose, but ravenous for knowledge, I know. He read the twelve volumes of my *Children's Encyclopaedia* over and over in the quiet afternoons. Regaling the customers at opening time with the bits he thought they would enjoy like 'I often wonder what the vintners buy one half so precious as the stuff they sell.'

In the morning, tapping barrels and emptying spittoons, he sang hymns with unhibited gusto. 'The common round, the daily task can furnish all I need to ask.' I wonder if it did. For he had another favourite quotation from the *Children's Encyclopaedia*: 'A longing she hardly dared to own for something better than she had known.'

The war was a godsend to the place and people. There was work in munitions and customers came speckled with what looked like gold-dust and might have been gun powder. Everyone suddenly had a lighter run up on a munitions lathe and nobody bought clay pipes any more at a penny apiece or cigarettes singly. Everybody had money and spent it like Scotsmen. I considered the Scots prodigious spenders. When they came in coachloads for a football match, they drank only doubles and those with such speed and ease that one barman was detailed off to pull corks all night.

The bundles of notes I carried up to the bank were thicker and stickier — when the till was full they were pushed into a pint-pot — and the bags of pennies I brought back were a dead weight. I was disgruntled too about being pressed into service as a glass washer at weekends. Only cold water would clean the glasses and by the end of the night my hands were numb. I thought Herrick's prayer appropriate. 'Here a little child I stand, heaving up my either hand; cold as paddocks though they be, here I lift them up to Thee.' Though little hardly described me now, the pathos of it pleased me.

I liked choosing the records for the radiogram though. George Formby, Gracie Fields, Flanagan and Allen and one, bought possibly for its thirst-inducing qualities, about 'Old Dan and I with throats burned dry and souls that cry for water. Cool, clear water.' Nobody listened but then I consoled myself nobody listened to Churchill either. Those films showing people with pints frozen halfway to their lips as they gathered round the radio puzzled me. Churchill's rallying calls were played over the loudspeaker but the only comment I ever heard was that he'd been at the bottle again. A most unwarranted conclusion drawn from his characteristically slurred delivery.

Liverpool burned in the night sky and my grandmother, being old and tenacious of life, kept a gas-mask beside her chamberpot to wear during alerts. My mother told the billeting officer we could take five cockneys and a hundred Canadians arrived.

They varied from the nice, polite one, who played what we took to be classical music because you couldn't sing to it hour after dreamy hour, to the one who fell downstairs in his cups, his underpants and the grandfather clock. It was after midnight and the uproar was such that my grandmother thought she'd missed the alert and put on her gas-mask.

Extrovert humanity boiled around me but I was too much alone. The pub was asleep when I went to school because publicans who work till early morning, clearing up and cashing up, don't get up at eight. In the evening walking through the roaring warmth, sober and shy, was a most solitary sensation.

Publicans don't have Sunday off. Or Christmas Day. Or any day. I must have been a docile child for I only created once.

I leaned over the banisters in my nightdress while the singing and smoke rose up and my tears plopped down. I was crying because I had waited to bring the New Year in and it was long after midnight. The beer pumps were covered with towels, the waiters were swiping unattended glasses and 'Time, gentlemen, please' had changed to a more urgent 'Nah then lads and lasses.'

I sobbed all the way downstairs and stood outside the front door which was ritually closed after me. One last reveller was sitting on the frozen sets singing 'Roll out the barrel'. He focused with some difficulty. 'Nay, they've nivver chucked thee out too, lass?' He hammered on the door and bellowed through the letter-box, 'Tha silly buggers . . .' The door opened abruptly and he fell in. My mother mopped my face and gave me a mince pie. 'You really brought the New Year in. He doesn't count. Everything's all right.'

But I hadn't. And he did. And it wasn't.

I didn't know then I was lonely but perhaps my parents did. For, with the pub's booming profits, they sent me to a very haughty southern boarding school. The term I was accepted the school was evacuated to a northern hotel.

❁

'Would I were in an alehouse in London! I would give all my fame for a pot of ale, and safety.'

WILLIAM SHAKESPEARE

Henry V

❁❁

Any man who has ever cursed our curious licensing laws, as which of us has not, has had a friend in Sir Alan Herbert. He may not have won all his battles but he didn't lose them all . . .

A. P. Herbert

THE PUB IN PARLIAMENT

The House of Commons, they say, is not respected as it was. There are even those who would destroy or tinker with the House of Lords. But the public house has marvellously improved its quality and status in my own life-time. I have lived in the same house at Hammersmith for fifty-three years. I have been using my 'local', the Black Lion, since the Twenties. In those days, among the respectable, 'public house' was almost a term of abuse. Some of the old ladies who peep behind curtains used to say, they told me, as I took my punctual evening walk, 'Do you see that man? He goes to that tavern nearly every day of his life!' I am glad to say that, whenever at home, the same habit has held me for nearly fifty years.

From 1934, too, I can call similar evidence. In that year, at the request of Sir John Reith, no less, still Director-General of the B.B.C., I wrote a series of sixteen talks, or rather scenes, called *Mr Pewter Works It Out*. Mr Pewter was an honest working-class pub-goer with robust opinions about everything. He had a wife and a daughter, and the daughter had a leftist young man. (I never saw the famous Alf Garnett but I gather that he had the same sort of cast.) The Pewters, I do believe, were the pioneers of all the Talking Families, the Dales, the Archers, and the rest. But far from treading delicately, as most of them do, my instructions were to let the Pewters tackle any controversial topic of the day, and say what they thought. They did, and the tackling was often pretty strong. But all went well until Scene 11, when Mr Pewter was put to bed. Worse, they refused to fetch him a pint from his local. Worse still, someone described his beer as 'alcoholic liquor'. In a fury, he read them a letter to the Press by four or five doctors about the number of babies who had perished from drinking tubercular milk. 'Give a dog a bad name!' he cried. 'How would you like it if I called your milk a "tuberculous beverage"?' Next morning the island wires were hot with protest. The National Milk Marketing Board were conducting a special campaign, and resented Mr Pewter richly. The end was a pleasant interview with Sir John Reith. He stood by us stoutly in the storm, and the series continued to its appointed end. But, I remember, when I expressed my view that the public house was a valuable institution he looked at me in surprise and said, 'But, Herbert, you don't go into pubs, do you?' Certainly, I said. It was the one true home of the classless society, and in a new place the stranger's best way to the mind of the people and the news of the day. 'Well,' he said temperately, 'on my way to this building I pass one or two, and I can only say that if I saw one of my staff coming out of one of them I should be disturbed.' I am not mocking Sir John, I have always admired him. I am simply recording that in 1934 this was the status of the pub — a place to which nice people did not go.

Not only the pubs but those who provided these places of refreshment, the brewers, were spoken of as public mischiefs. My old friend Nancy, Lady Astor, would hiss insults about *The Trade* as if they were the Slave Trade of long ago, or the Drug Peddler today. In 1934, the year before I joined her in the House of Commons, I went to Bow Street, in cold blood, on a Monday morning, and laid an 'information' against the Kitchen Committee of the House of Commons for selling drink without a licence and without attention to the statutory 'hours'. The mad notion was that if Parliament had to obey the same mad laws as the citizen they might at least consider amending them. I was defeated, of course, after two expensive days in the High Court (Attorney-General and all): but Lord Hewart, the Lord Chief Justice, thought so much of my case that the Crown had to pay their own costs. (I doubt if ever again a humble citizen will prosecute the House of Commons at a personal cost of £45.) One day, while collecting 'evidence', I attended a Standing Committee meeting on some Licensing Bill or other (as any citizen may do) and I took with me the late George Izzard, landlord of the Dove, Hammersmith. Afterwards I met Nancy Astor who was on the Committee. I told her my purpose, and asked her to buy me a drink at Annie's Bar, which I could use as evidence. She would thus help to drive the Demon Drink from Parliament. But, to her credit, more faithful to Parliament than to her principles, she good-humouredly refused. But then, with a sort of venom she said, 'Who was that with you? One of *The Trade* — I could see that at once' — as if it was improper for a 'publican' to take an interest in the laws concerning pubs.

Somewhere, by the way, perhaps in Annie's Bar, there should be a memorial plaque in my honour, for my mad prosecution firmly established, free from doubt, and secured for ever, the unique liberties of Parliament in these affairs. There had been a lot of talk about Parliament being immune from the Licensing Acts because it sat in the Palace of Westminster which was 'a Royal Palace'. But, as my advisers predicted, this argument was not considered in Court. Lord Hewart, prompted by Mr

Justice Avory, snatched at a passage in Lord Denman's judgment in the famous case of Stockdale *v.* Hansard:

> The Commons of England are not invested with more power and dignity by their legislative character than by that which they have as the grand inquest of the nation. *All the privileges that can be required for the energetic discharge of the duties inherent in that high trust are conceded without a murmur or a doubt.*

So the decision rested firmly on Parliamentary privilege, and if the House is burned down again and Parliament meets in the Albert Hall, the Licensing Acts will still not 'be applicable'. It is necessary, note, for the 'energetic discharge' of the Members' duties that the consumption of 'intoxicating liquor' shall be uncontrolled. Quite a different view is taken about consumption by the ordinary citizen — but never mind. I think I deserve my plaque.

In the following year, before I had even thought of standing for Parliament, one of *The Trade,* the ancient firm of Younger's, asked if I would contribute, for a pleasant fee, an article to some sort of magazine they were preparing. I wrote a piece showing the gross difference between the taxes paid by the beasts who 'drink' and smoke and the virtuous souls who don't. Before the magazine was ready I was, to cosmic astonishment, elected one of the two 'Burgesses', or Members of Parliament, for Oxford University. I wrote to *The Trade* and said I hoped that they would still use the article, if they liked it, but they must not pay me anything for it. 'You know how careful Members have to be,' I said. I was thinking of one of dear Nancy's grand parties at St James' Square. She was receiving her guests at the top of the great stair, surrounded by admiring ambassadors and statesmen, my wife and I (white tie, tails, and all) were shyly climbing the stairs. Half-way up I heard her loud clear voice cry, 'Here comes the grog-blossom! Here comes the brewer's friend!' I always admired Nancy for her wit and courage, and though her rudeness, I sometimes felt, was slightly overdone, it was not the custom to resent it. I did not mind being called 'the brewer's friend', but now, in my new capacity, she must not be able to say that I was 'in the brewers' pay', as she did of almost everyone who argued with her. Younger's wrote that they quite understood, and no doubt I should hear from the Chairman later, he was away. Weeks later, without a word of warning, a large van drew up outside, and there emerged the thirteen vast volumes of the *Oxford English Dictionary*, beautifully bound in red morocco. I have been using it ever since: and I thought it such a delicate, imaginative gift from one of the gross-minded, contemptible *Trade* that I wished Nancy was there to see it.

It was chance, not this beautiful bribe, which caused my second Commons speech to be on '*Trade*' affairs. A Private Member's Licensing (Amendment) Bill came up in March 1936. One purpose was to 'standardise' the hours of 'opening', especially in London, to end the ugly rush from Borough A, where the pubs closed at 10.30, into Borough B, where 'the hour' was 11.0; another was to deal with 'the bogus club'. Even this simple and sensible sort of reform was opposed in those days by the 'temperance' brigade, as reluctant to improve the pub world as a Labour statesman to reform the House of Lords. The worse the enemy was the better.

I followed Dr Salter, a savage temperance man, I see (*Hansard,* 6 March 1936, Col. 1724):

> I suppose that in the public life of this land there could be no more moving spectacle than that which we have had this morning, of a fierce teetotaller,

PUB

whom I congratulate upon his sincerity . . . shedding hot tears over the hard lot of the unhappy barmaid, and even putting in a good word for the poor publican. I think that his is a slightly disingenuous plea, because the hon. Member knows very well that if the Bill contained a provision for a 36-hour week for the barmaid he would still oppose it. He knows, too, that if the Bill be passed into law the barmaid and the barman will still be in a superior position to the waiter at the temperance hotel, to whom the Shop Hours Acts do not apply.

'What is a pub?' I asked the startled House (Col. 1726) and I replied:

I was very glad to hear at last a good word about the pub from the hon. Member for Eddisbury. He was quite right.

Mr R. J. Russell, seconding the opposition to the Bill, had said:

I know that for many years I have been an object of suspicion by my temperance friends because I cannot take a very narrow view on this question. *I have always believed, and still believe that there is a real social service to be taken up and carried on by the village inn, a service of recreation and fellowship, which could be made a great instrument for human betterment.*'

This utterance, coming from the temperance world, was like a new planet in the sky. I developed it:

Forgetting the large gin palaces which we see sometimes in our main streets, we can agree that the pub is, on the whole, a social centre and, I suggest, a very valuable social institution. It is a centre to which people can go for political sanity and, for temperance purposes, it is the instrument of control. It is a place where people who do not own rich houses, who have

195

no billiard rooms or gardens of their own, are able to go for social intercourse, to discuss the troubles of life and the news of the day. I would ask hon. Members, in discussing this question, to remember that the public house is not a sink of iniquity, and that the publican is not a man who wants to ruin his fellow countrymen. It is said in the trade that it is more difficult to become a publican than a parson. He has to give seven years' good character; every minute of his life for seven years is gone into.

I went on:

Dr Salter told us that there is drunkenness, and increasing drunkenness, and I am not surprised; but he did not give us the real cause. I say without hesitation that, if there is drunkenness, and if there is increasing drunkenness, it is the temperance party, and the licensing justices above all, who are responsible for a great deal of it. They complain, perhaps rightly, that wherever a redundant house, as they call it — what a word! — that is to say, an unnecessary house, a needless house, is closed, a bogus club springs up; but, if a bogus club springs up where formerly there was a licensed house, does not that show that the licensed house was not redundant? The club has met a need which really existed, but without the control to which the public house is subject; it *is really an uncontrolled public house.* That is one cause of increasing drunkenness and the houses that are described as redundant are generally the smaller ones with an atmosphere, with a tradition, with skittles and darts, and their customers are driven to the big gin palace in the High Street or to the bogus club. [Col. 1727.] Many — I do not say all — licensing benches do a great deal of harm by opposing improvement, because they think that improvement will bring more people to the public house which is what they call the drinking area, and so they themselves perpetuate the system of the public house being merely a drinking place and nothing else. For this and many other reasons I say that the licensing justices, and the temperance party, are responsible for much of the drunkenness that exists, and if they oppose this or any other Bill they will be continuing their work in that direction. Hon. Gentlemen here are indignant when it is said, but we all know it is true, that, while nobody may sit on a licensing bench who has any interest in the trade, biased members of the temperance party can and do sit on these benches. All the rest of the year they very often do no work at all as justices, but when the Brewster Sessions come round they crawl out from every hole and corner and crowd on to the benches. I can give an example of the kind of thing they will do. There is a quiet, respectable old public house near where I live. It has a garden, where, on Saturday nights, and particularly on hot Saturday nights in the summer, people with no gardens of their own congregate with their wives, families and dogs. The landlord desired to give them a little music on Saturday evenings. He applied to the London County Council for a music licence, and he got it, with the very proper proviso that he should move a door from one position to another, in order that there might be a safe exit in case of fire. He then had to go to the licensing justices who have to pass all structural alterations, because the moving of this door from one position to another was a structural alteration. The Kensington licensing justices, who are notoriously the worst bench in the world, and who were responsible for the 10 o'clock closing about which complaints were being made the other day, said: 'What is this? Music will bring more people into the drinking area'; and so they refused permission to move the door and turned the whole thing down, not on its merits, but because they were determined that that house should never be improved and no one should ever go there if they could help it. It is that kind of thing which causes one to say that the licensing justices in many places — I do not say everywhere — are not discharging their functions properly, and I think the system is one which ought to be swept away. It is one of the merits of this Bill that it would take away from them some of their discretion. [Col. 1728.]

It was complained that the Bill did not follow the recommendation of the most recent Royal Commission, and I had something to say about that (Col. 1730):

I have this interesting document, the Report of the Royal Commission, here, and looking at the index I see not only the entry 'Temperance bars, alleged abuses in', but also this alarming entry 'Trains, drunkenness in'. When I turn to the page indicated, expecting to read of hideous orgies on the 9.15, I find there is *no* drunkenness in trains, that there have been *no* complaints, and that 'the service of intoxicants outside the restaurant car has not led to any abuses'. But this did not prevent the Commission from recommending some new restrictions. That is the kind of report that this is. There are some sensible things in it, but always we find restriction for restriction's sake. This Royal Commission actually recommends that all licensed premises with the exception of hotels and restaurants shall be closed at 10 o'clock. Here in the heart of the Empire one would not even be able to get a glass of port or a glass of beer during the second interval of a play.

I concluded:

My mind goes back to a year ago, when I was naughtily and boldly laying information against the Kitchen Committee of this House. There was not then lighthearted talk about 'intoxicating liquor' and about 'liberty which nobody wanted'. There was indignation, and rightly. This House did not then say, 'Oh, well, these things do not really matter, let us have more control, let us obey the law which we have imposed on the people.' This House marched out to battle— horse, foot, and Attorney-General — to defend its rights and privileges, and I congratulate them. I am very glad that they succeeded. The High Court decided that continual access to refreshment of every kind was essential to the conduct of the business of this House, although the business of this House is the most important business of making laws. I do not say that people demand the same privileges as there are in this House — I think they are glad that this House has special privileges — but they would like to have the same spirit shown in this House when their simple human desires are being considered. [*Independent Member,* Methuen.]

It was not a bad speech, I think, bright in tone but serious in intent and founded on fact. But Viscountess Astor, in her long speech, could only say, 'I am not going to deal with the hon. Member for Oxford University because we know that he is the playboy of the drink world.'

This was the first of our ludicrous clashes. According to *Hansard* I interrupted in unseemly fashion:

May I suggest that a regular course of narcotics would be extremely good for the Noble Lady? She would be a less restless Member.
Viscountess Astor: The Noble Lady will be restless in this House long after the hon. Member for Oxford University. [But she wasn't.] I am not going to deal seriously with him because we know that he has a picture of the old-fashioned pub where there is music

and merriment and good cheer. It is a beautiful
picture. I only wish it were true. If it were not for the
vested interests of the drink trade it would be true,
but those conditions are long past.'

The Home Secretary (Sir John Simon) made a discouraging speech, as Ministers generally did on a Private
Members' Friday: but he said 'definitely that it is the
intention of the Government next Sessoin to introduce a
Bill to deal with bogus clubs.'

The promoter thereupon withdrew his Bill; but the
Government did not, I think, introduce a Bill of their
own in the next Session.

Still, 'Say not the struggle naught availeth'. Many
years later many of the things proposed by the 'grog-
blossom', the 'vested interests', etc., that day were done.
'Hours' were standardised, the bogus club was tackled,
members of *The Trade*, if magistrates, were no longer
excluded from the Brewster Sessions, proposed 'improvements' stood a better chance and hotels and restaurants
at last received some special civilised facilities.

I was never a blind uncritical friend of '*The Trade*'. In
those old days there was many an uncomely and uncom-
fortable 'inn' in London which offered nothing but
'booze', not a bed, not a sandwich, not so much as a
dartboard, and deserved some at least of Nancy's nasty
remarks. I said to many a friendly publican, 'You're a
"licensed victualler", you know. Where are the victuals?'
In 1943, I see, I dragged this matter into the debate on the
Second Reading of Mr Ernest Bevin's Catering (Wages)
Bill. I admired and liked 'Ernie', but I thought his Bill
was cumbrous and ill-conceived and far from likely to
help 'the efficiency and development' of the overtaxed
and harassed industries, as the Preamble proclaimed. I
refused to vote for it and think I was right. My pompous

opening, I feel, deserves a medal (*Hansard,* 9 February 1943, Col. 1253):

> Mr Speaker, Sir, historians, who are often unfair, may remark with sardonic interest that at a time when the whole of Europe is waiting to hear the thunder of the guns of the united nations and to see the ships bringing food to the starving peoples, the House of Commons was compelled, even bullied by His Majesty's Government to discuss a contentious Measure concerning eating and drinking in Great Britain — after the war. I should not share that view. These things are important in the life of the nation. The way in which they are conducted is an index not only of our civilisation but of our character and even of the soul of a nation. They are a corner of the art of life, and therefore suitable, I think, for the attention of a University Member.

All this led up to one more ridiculous bicker with Nancy Astor. For once, I thought, I was saying things that would please her:

> I gather that the Minister of Labour 'desires to see the British inn compete with the Continent in the provision of decent meals and beds!' I should like to see it too. Much as I have said, and fought, and written for the people's beer, and the people's pub, I agree that there is much that is barbarous in our conditions, and if those conditions were likely to be swept away by the Bill I should support it. I hate to see a mother and child standing in the rain, or even in the sun, outside a place of refreshment which the law has decided is not fit for a child under sixteen to enter. I hate to take anybody into a place labelled 'licensed victualler' when I know that you will not be able to get any 'victuals' there at all — not so much as a sausage roll (though let me say, this is better than it was — I know many a little pub which has done very well, but they are far

> between). I hate to take a foreigner, a Parisian for example, into an eating-house, where I have to confess that the wines of this country are taxed as though they were dangerous poisons.
> *Mr Speaker:* I hope that the hon. and gallant Member will not get on to the subject of the licensing laws.
> *Petty-Officer Herbert:* The licensing laws were mentioned in the Amendment which I had on the Paper.
> *Mr Speaker:* That is one of the reasons why I did not select that Amendment.

Very discouraging. But I laboured on:

> I was trying to examine what the Bill will do for the efficiency and development of the industry. What I want to see, and I know what the right hon. Gentleman wants to see, is more cheap decent eating-houses for the people where not merely man and wife but man, wife, and child can go and entertain themselves together — as they can in almost any street abroad . . . There are not enough. (*Interruption*)

Lady Astor was muttering away behind me in the way that used to madden Mr Churchill, when he sat on the same bench. Now I turned on her:

'Do let me implore the Noble Lady not to interrupt me even when I am agreeing with her.'

Then some devil snatched up from my 'sub-conscious' our earliest encounter:

'Four years ago [no, it was seven years] I gave her the advice to take a barrel of port every day to soothe her nerves and make her a better citizen and a less restless Member of Parliament.'

Not very funny, I agree, but the House laughed loudly — so many of them had suffered from Nancy's slings and arrows. Instead of sitting quiet she rose in her place, and I 'gave way':

PUB

Viscountess Astor: Does the Hon. and gallant Member think that those people who take a barrel of port every day are better Members than me in this House?

Members roared again at this comical query.

Petty-Officer Herbert: I have never had that experience. My only doubt about the Noble Lady is whether a barrel would be a sufficient sedative.

Ungallant, inelegant, no doubt: but it was always 'No Quarter' between us. At least we caused amusement, and my old friend was silent for a whole column of *Hansard*.

Today the 'licensed victualler' is a true title almost everywhere. There can be few pubs which do not provide food of some sort, if it is only sandwiches or sausage-rolls. Many give excellent hot lunches or substantial snacks, my own local included. But that made necessary an extension of the premises, 'structural alterations', which had to have the consent of the licensing justices. In the bad old days of which I have written I believe that consent might have been refused, on the ancient ground that 'the drinking area' would be augmented and the food would draw more citizens to the perilous place.

All this 'victualling' is a splendid revolution. The children still cannot victual with their parents at a pub — but that is the fault of the laws of Parliament (and we must remember that not every parent wants to be bothered by his progeny at the pub).

Quietly the wicked *Trade* have been fathering other revolutions. Elegance and Comfort marching hand in hand. Ancient inns preserved and fortified, but with new insides, decoration and fittings. The careful encouragement of good inn-signs, of good lettering on the walls, good glasses, pretty bars and gardens. Art is much more in the minds of the contemptible *Trade* than ever it was in

Nancy Astor's legions. Whitbread's, to name one firm alone, have won special credit as patrons of the arts — the fine *Whitbread Almanac,* for example, prepared each year by commissioned painters and writers.

I have one faint uneasiness about some of the improvements and reforms. They may, to some extent, militate against my 'classless society' claims. The simple 'local', smartened up, may grow into a 'road-house', more prosperous but not the same. The businessman's lunch-tables may drive out the countryman's dartboard and the working man too. When the division between Saloon and Public Bar is removed the result may be not more democratic but less. Twenty years ago, I was sometimes proud to be chosen to play for the Black Lion first skittles team (eight players) against the Full Moon, Chelsea, or the Waterman at Putney. Nearly all the others were ordinary working men with early jobs in the morning, and grand company they were. One of them, Chris Jackson (I can see him now), was a sewer man, and one night, after he had won his game in a match, he opened a hole in the road outside the pub and took me down to see his sewer. For many a year the Champion Cup sat on the shelf above the Black Lion bar. This kind of thing never entered the heads of the Nancy Astors. It was the sort of myth imagined by 'the playboy': and besides, if it was true, would it not draw more victims into 'the drinking area'?

It is not the fault of the brewers and their 'vested interests' that Black Lion skittles is no more. Indeed, two years back, when there was talk of a big reconstruction, the brewers, Watneys, kindly showed me the architect's plans: they included a spacious semi-basement space for 'a new skittle alley'. *The Trade* have their eyes open, and will be watchful, I am sure, for their classless society.

No doubt there is still much to be done 'in the drink world', but what has been done is a wonder, and it has been done, as I have shown, with grudging help from Parliament and in battle with the Nancy Astors.

But I was glad in 1940 to blow that bold lady a Parliamentary kiss. She was muttering loudly behind me as usual while I spoke. But this time I turned and said, 'I have so much admiration for the brave work which the Noble Lady the Member for the Sutton Division of Plymouth has been doing in her constituency that I hope she will not provoke me into making a sharp reply to her.'

Later, in the same year, when I transferred from the London River Emergency Service to the Royal Naval Auxiliary (Thames) Patrol I was proud to be marked 'A 1' at the Admiralty medical examination. The grog-blossom sent a wire to his friend Harry Strauss (now Lord Conesford) at the House:

> PASSED AI FOR NAVY FIFTY THIS YEAR PLEASE TELL NANCY.

Down the river in Sea Reach I got this nice reply:

> MUST BE SOMETHING WRONG WITH NAVY NANCY.

We dined at an excellent inn at Chapel-house, where he
expatiated on the felicity of England in its taverns and
inns, and triumphed over the French for not having, in
any perfection, the tavern life. 'There is no private house,
(said he), in which people can enjoy themselves so well, as
at a capital tavern . . . He then repeated, with great
emotion, Shenstone's lines:

> Whoe'er has travell'd life's dull round,
> Where'er his stages may have been,
> May sigh to think he still has found
> The warmest welcome at an inn.

JAMES BOSWELL

The Life of Samuel Johnson

> For on this my heart is set:
> When the hour is nigh me,
> Let me in the tavern die,
> With a tankard by me,
> While the angels looking down
> Joyously sing o'er me,
> Deus sit propitius
> Huic potatori.

Anonymous (twelfth century)
translated from the Latin
by Helen Waddell

I confess I lost my temper yesterday at Rotterdam, where I had to pay a florin for a bottle of ale (the water not being drinkable, and country or Bavarian beer not being genteel enough for the hotel); I confess, I say, that my fine temper was ruffled, when the bottle of pale ale turned out to be a pint bottle; and I meekly told the waiter that I had bought beer at Jerusalem at a less price. But then Rotterdam is eighteen hours from London, and the steamer with the passengers and beer comes up to the hotel windows; whilst to Jerusalem they have to carry the ale on camels' backs from Beyrout or Jaffa, and through hordes of marauding Arabs, who evidently don't care for pale ale, though I am told it is not forbidden in the Koran. Mine would have been very good, but I choked with rage whilst drinking it. A florin for a bottle, and that bottle having the words 'imperial pint', in bold relief, on the surface! It was too much. I intended not to say anything about it; but I *must* speak. A florin a bottle, and that bottle a pint! Oh, for shame! for shame! I can't cork down my indignation; I froth up with fury; I am pale with wrath, and bitter with scorn.

WILLIAM MAKEPEACE THACKERAY

Notes of a Week's Holiday

⚙⚙

James Cameron could well be the world's most travelled writer. His years as a foreign correspondent have taken him from war to war, crisis to crisis, each one, or so it has seemed to him, further from his local than the last. That, as has already been observed, is the trouble with other countries. Leave these shores and you are more than likely to find yourself in a world without pubs . . .

James Cameron

BUT, OH, THE PUBLESS YEARS ...

Have you ever tried to get a drink on the long Tibetan road between Yatung and Lhasa? No? Neither have I; let us modify our pretensions. But I have tried to get a drink in Kansas, and in Madras, and in Saudi Arabia, and I did serve several months in the United States Navy. All dry, dry as bones. *But how did you get ON, daddy?* Well, child, it's a long story . . .

The world is broad, and by and large I dare say it has about as many pubs as it needs. Unfortunately they are *not always in the right places.* In Ireland, for example, where I spend all the time I can, there is in most inhabited places a pub roughly every fourteen feet. If it is not a pub it is a grocer's or a corn-chandler's or a sock-shop or a fish-monger, most of which establishments tend to have a Counter in the Corner. It is very hard in West Ireland to get through ten minutes at a time without a something to help the day along.

This of course is all very well, because Ireland is not a place where one works. Twice in my life I have gone over to West Cork to finish a book — ah, the peace, the silence, the absence of interruption; whizzo, four thousand words a day. Not on your nellie. After an hour and a half of this creative paradise one lifts one's eyes from one's paper with the gnawing thought: why am I the *only* individual in the whole of this Republic who is doing any work this fair day?

So one goes to have a little check up down the road, and sure enough there are all the boyos in the grocer's helping the day along, and there goes another unfinished book.

In a life that has not been wholly without a certain variety of movement and experience I long ago came to arrange my memories, and later even to plot my course, in close relationship to those places where I would be fed and watered. I began to serve my time as an itinerant bagman of journalism some time during the last war — I mean the one everyone calls the War; all the subsequent ones have been called something else — when, curiously enough, our own sceptr'd isle was just about the worst drinking country on earth. I do not know if you remember those punitive days when you had to be the publican's brother-in-law to get a drink at all, and to get another you had to own the mortgage.

PUB

It is not improbable that this was one of the factors that directed my attention to the business of becoming a foreign correspondent.

Thereafter I moved around at a great lick for some twenty-five years. It was a period of alarums and excursions, international fidgets, clarion calls, 48-point headlines and emergencies cancelling each other out at a rate of knots, and *very few pubs*.

Drinking places yes. One of my earliest duties was to appreciate that there are three wholly interlingual words, comprehensible from Samarkand to Streatham; they are *taxi* (tachsi, ТАКСИ, taks); *toilet* (toilette, *ТОАЛЕТ*); and especially *bar*. This is a universal ideogram, even the Russians call it БАР and the Greeks, even more eccentrically, *МПАР*. It can be disguised as taverna, Bierlokal, estaminet, bistro, zinco, or Abdullah's Divan. All these places have their value, God knows, but they are not and never were and nevermore shall be pubs.

I do not have to define pubs; they are to be found in England, even though in my view the brewers and the Travel Association tend to over-romanticise them and pretend they have the old quality. Swiftly disappearing as it is behind layers of crimson wallpaper and Musak, there are still enough of them to make it just possible to survive the other British institutions. Imagine an Order in Council that abolished them altogether!

It has happened elsewhere. I mentioned Madras, the onetime jewel in the Imperial throne. There is also Bombay Province. These were redoubts of some of the drinkingest men you ever heard of, the pillars of the Empire on which the sun set with such a bang in 1947. Bearer — eleven more burra-pegs and a pint of Murree. In comes Liberty, and in comes Prohibition. They started to examine you at the octroi for bottles. They even sometimes let down your tyres, and if your tyres squirted Scotch you were in trouble. This troublesome rite endures.

The thing could be circumvented, naturally. (*Everything* in Indian can be circumvented, given a long enough life.) Foreigners, being beyond the Hindu pale, could get a creepy thing called a Drinker's Licence. I have one dated in the 1950s; to obtain it, it was necessary to present oneself to the appropriate official and sign oneself on as an Addict. This was a humiliating process, but not disabling. You could require to be registered as an Addict in the First, Second, or Third Degree, each graduation entitling one an additional monthly Unit (which was their stern name for bottle). If you insisted upon the third category of Addiction (as obviously everyone did) they took away your driving-licence. Then you found that the stuff cost the sterling equivalent of about seven pounds a bottle.

When I frequented Bombay it was my custom to stay with my dear and evergreen friend, the late Mrs Krishna Hutheesing. She had this matter taped. On the way from the airport she would suggest that it would save time if one just nipped into the Permit Office on the way home. Once there, things went like lightning, since Krishna was the sister of the then Prime Minister, Mr Nehru, and consequently had a lot of *protectia,* as you can imagine. Within minutes I had my Addiction, my Permit, and was busy stocking up with half a dozen Units of stuff, say fifty quids' worth. This we escorted carefully home, and the next morning at dawn I always had to catch my plane to Delhi. Thus was my dear Krishna, rest her soul today, assured of a decent and steady norm of hospitality for her uncountable friends.

But, oh, the publess years. In them I am obliged to count my annual, and sometimes oftener, safari to the United States, where it is not for nothing that the word

PUB

'Saloon' was invented. 'Saloon'! — a splendid word, evocative of all manner of harsh and readymade conviviality, now untimely quenched under the tide of the unseemly 'cocktail-bar'. Long forgotten in England, it endures a thousandfold in the bleaker and opulent-arid empire of the small-town taverns and the chain-motels. These ill-lit caverns, these awful sombre grottoes designed at great expense to ensure that no man shall know who is his drinking-neighbour, nor indeed what he himself is drinking. Those chattering glasses of whisky-flavoured ice; those lethal doses of solid-and-a-hint-of vermouth! Ask not to meet a friend in these Stygian cellars; you will both be plastered long before you see the whites of each other's eyes.

Pub-life in America, to be sure, is a specialised subject. It is indeed a generation since the Volstead Act was repealed, but there are still places in the U.S. where you cannot get a drink — for money anyhow; I don't know about love. Not long ago I spent a weekend in Arkansas: just *try* to get a glass of beer there on a Sunday. Might as well be in Aberystwyth. Even worse; Aberystwyth never had 104 degrees of heat. I once did an enormous train-ride clean across the U.S. from Washington to California (don't tell me it can't be done; this was a thing called the Crossroads Special, bound for Bikini) and roughly every four hours we ran into new State Legislation, with glasses being whipped off and on the table like the three-card trick. Or have you ever blundered through the provincial drink-laws in our great friend and neighbour, Canada? Here you can buy a drink and take it home; here you can't; here you may take a lady and here you can't; here you can drink standing up and here sitting down. No wonder the Canadians are so upstanding, clear-eyed, and dull.

We haven't all that much to be proud of either. I come from Scotland, which until not long ago had the peculiar reputation of distributing the good stuff all over the world, at no small reward to them, while making it uncommonly awkward to get your hands on it at home. (This is still to some degree true.) Until a few years ago when enlightenment briefly shone around the land there was an inhuman law in Scotland that forbade public drinking in Scotland on Sunday to everyone who was not a *bona-fide traveller*; this preposterous rule meant that you could buy a drink in any licensed premises five miles (I think it was five miles) from where you lived, but nowhere else. What this silly law was all in aid of I never learned, but there it was and I lived under it. It meant, for example, that in the adjacent townships of Forfar and Kirriemuir, a few miles apart, there was every Sabbath a simple transfer of populations. On Sunday if you wanted anyone from Forfar you caught them in Kirriemuir, and vice versa. The same nonsense was going on all over Scotland, I am sorry to say.

Well — it came to pass that during the late hostilities in Korea, if anyone remembers that far back, I got myself released from a grisly place called Taegu, and thus to Itchikawa in Japan, and Tokyo, and homewards by way of Saigon and Singapore and Delhi and Karachi and God knows where finally back to Glasgow, where it seems I lived. In those days it took forever.

Somehow ultimately I shuddered into the station hotel there and, at peace at last, asked for a drink. Would I please sign the book? Gladly. Uselessly. I was in a Glasgow pub; my address was Glasgow. I was not *bona-fide*. I had only just accomplished eleven thousand miles across the hemispheres, I knew neither whether it was day or night, yesterday or tomorrow, but in the eyes of the law

PUB

I was *not a traveller*. No drink for papa. How vigorously at that moment did I wish triumph to the Scottish Nationalists, so that they could achieve Statehood, so that I could there and then have renounced it.

If you ever want to be kept on the wagon by experts, I recommend you to join the aforesaid United States Navy. For reasons that I suppose seem proper to the U.S. Navy Department, all vessels of that Fleet, from the enormous carrier *Enterprise* to the titsiest pinnace, abide by the provisions of the long-dead Volstead Act; that is to say they maintain strict prohibition. (This, needless to say, is in marked contrast to the Royal Navy.) For the U.S. sailors it is Coca Cola all the way. The dispiriting effect is hard to describe. It is not that one misses the tot; it is that the day itself loses shape, it has no punctuation marks. Come six o'clock there is nothing to do. The sun sinks over the yardarm unsaluted. Another cup of coffee is somehow not the same thing.

The inevitable consequence of this is that when the Fleet is ashore it goes barmy. Deprived of practice, it drinks immoderately. Sometimes the situation can become bizarre. I well recall being with a ship's company that was put ashore on the small atoll of Bikini, in the Pacific Marshall Islands, which in those days had connotations other than swimsuits. On the atoll there was an officers' club (their word for bar) which was made of palm-leaf thatch and was most regrettably called the Up and Atom. What the hell; we repaired to it willingly enough. Because of the exceptional circumstances of that evening, a very curious house rule was in operation. The bar, for which the morrow would bring the most definitive and final of all closing-times, was full of stuff that was expendable in the truest sense. It was ordained therefore that one's first drink cost sixty cents, one's second fifty, one's third forty, and so on; after half a dozen it was on the house. Fantastic state of affairs! None of us had had so much as a smell of a cork for five weeks. Talk about a party.

At eight o'clock the following morning they dropped an Atom Bomb on the joint and blew it to kingdom come.

Have you ever risen with a hangover to the sound of an Atom Bomb?

There just aren't any words.

A world without pubs. Well, I don't know. Up until the 1950s there wasn't, as far as I know, a pub in all Moscow. This was odd, or so it seemed to me, since the Muscovites are a notably convivial crowd, though their drinking ritual was seldom impromptu. It went through a difficult period after Mr Khrushchev was taken off the hard stuff and tried to get everybody else taken off it too, but it survived. Nevertheless there seemed to be no pubs in the accepted sense. I claim a very small credit for one innovation. A friend and I were in the habit of frequenting the big Gastronom shop in Gorky Street to buy a flask of vodka and some of that effervescent sugar-alley water the Russians call champagne, but then we had of course to find somewhere to drink it. Twenty years of hotel bedrooms have never persuaded me that they are good places for this. On impulse, then, we asked the management of the Gastronom if they would put up a little shelf and a couple of stools. They did. Subject to expert correction, I believe that to have been the very first pub in Gorky Street. Today, when you go and knock back your elevenses in the smart Foreign Currency Cocktail Lounge in the Hotel Nationale, you can have one on me. But it won't be the same.

How one goes on about pubs. Everyone I know has

this thing about the world's Famous Bars. The legends are put about by newspapermen and the like — rightly in a way, because it is the case that almost everywhere there is a *place* to which these people gravitate for the dissemination of rumours and professional bullshit. No one knows exactly why this pub is more acceptable than that, but there it is — the Cockpit in Singapore, Bleick's in New York or Charley O's, the Paris Crillon, the Cosmo in Cairo, the Ledra Palace in Cyprus, and so on. Perhaps it has something to do with getting tick. A world without them would be an eerie place.

That brings us to the Longest Bar In The World. There is one of these in several places I know. Probably the most celebrated, and for all I know the longest, was in Shanghai. It has of course gone, untimely quenched by the tide of history. I think I was one of its very last customers. I had somehow wandered down from the puritan austerities of Peking to watch the ghosts of old International Shanghai, and there I found the old Cathay Hotel cryptically renamed the King Kong, where the old Long Bar was still, but desultorily and only just, in business. I think it must have been the very last real bar left in China. There were two dismal Czechs holed up somewhere in the shadows, nobody else. It seemed the place was about to be converted to an annexe of the Youth Pioneers' Committee Hall, and serve it right.

There now is a publess world: China. I am devoted to China more than to anywhere, probably, but it must be admitted that this is a serious strike against it. The Chinese are not anti drinking, far from it, which says something for them considering the terrible stuff they have to drink. They have this routine, however, which many people claim is so civilised but which I have my doubts about, of drinking only when dining. Then they partake copiously of this *huang-chou*, which is hot rice wine with singularly little therapeutic value for me. They compensate for this with a liquor of lethal ferocity called *mao t'ai*, which is carried around in bottles made of granite. Presumably it would dissolve anything else.

But of pubs China has none. I travelled some twenty thousand miles through that great land and never once got my elbow on a piece of wood. I am not sure there is not room for yet another Cultural Revolution.

I often wonder what the poor foreigners would have done without us. The fanciful stuff they drink on their own! The Russians have the *kvass* (which is made out of *bread*, if you please), the Mexicans *tequila*, the Turks *raki*, the Japanese *sake*, the Tibetans *chang* (nobody knows what *that* is made of), the Peruvians *pisco*, and so on and so on and so on. The French of course have wine, but to the last I will deny that this has any place in pubs. In Hanoi they make a nightmare brew called *liu moi*. The brave Vietnamese both drink it and fill their lighters with it. If ever there was a place where one needed a drink it was Hanoi, and that is what happens.

Somehow or other one always gets by . . .

A world without pubs, Not yet, thank God.

'One bitter, one mild and one merger.'

❂❂

*The brewing industry has thrown up its own aristocracy. There are
the hereditary peers, the great families who have brewed the
nation's beer for generations and whose names have become household
words. Then there are the life peers, strong men who have risen to
the board room from the ranks. Together they make the formidable
and powerful force that has been called the Beerage.*

David Jenkins

❂❂❂

THE BEERAGE

'All happy families resemble each other.' — Tolstoy

Folded into some ungainly side-street of most towns and cities of Britain, there will usually be a peculiarly early-Victorian building, of an awkward four or five storeys. Originally constructed in red brick, it is now corroded by decades of sulphuric deposit. Its grandeur, with its fluted towers, whimsical stained-glass signs, pseudo-Gothic windows, papillas of stone, wealed and grimy gargoyles, is of an architectural obstinacy rarely paralleled. It is the town's brewery, often being run by the great-great-grandson of the founder, whose portrait, grave, upright, bearded, is the real chairman of the monthly board meetings. No matter what efforts are made to sandblast the grime away, no matter what damage caused by those conflicts that cannot be solved over a glass of the patron's brew, it remains immutably itself, an extraordinarily viable institution. Steeped in nineteenth-century pragmatism, it is yet eager to grasp that portion of twentieth-century progress that is most congenial to the founding spirit that pervades the building like the smell of a faithful old malt hopper.

It is in these industrial coverts that most breweries are content to stay, self-regenerative, self-defending, self-reliant. Occasionally, one is swallowed up to feed the territorial appetite of one of the bigger companies, or it just expires. But, in that each of them represents the status of the industry in society, and points to the origins of the fortunes of the great brewing families, they are the grass roots. It is from these seemingly shabby alleys in Burton, Southwark, the City of London, Newcastle, and Edinburgh, that the great families launched themselves, to reach a discreet pre-eminence, to become a powerful political lobby, a potent social and economic force, in a word, the Beerage.

With the possible exception of banking, no other industry is subject to such essentially family influence as brewing. Certainly no other industry of its size would collectively allow what it would consider the indulgence of family continuity. The industry, historically dominated by the fortunes of about a dozen families, is formidable. The total expenditure by the British in 1967 on liquor was £1,600 million. Of this, perhaps three-quarters was handled by the brewers. In terms of assets, brewing is seventh of the manufacturing industries, eighth of all industries including the retail sector, and tenth of all industrial and financial groupings in Britain. (In terms of tradition, the Brewers' Company, formed in the twelfth century, with St Thomas à Becket unaccountably as its patron saint, stands fourteenth among the eighty City of London companies, just after the Dyers in age, just older than the Leathersellers.) All the major brewing groups — and the top six account for about 70 per cent of the total production of the industry — still have members of the founding families on the board, usually as chairmen too. Although the actual holdings are declining, for various reasons, substantial amounts of family money are still tied up in the breweries. At least two of the major companies are family controlled. In three cases, the direct descendant of the founder of the firm is chairman, in another case, a direct descendant of a nineteenth-century partner holds the chair. And that is just among the top eight.

As a group, the Beerage bears some resemblance to the hereditary aristocracy, with its proprietorial solidity, its consciousness of its forebears, and its amorphous, yet respected, power outside its own province. At the same time, it draws many of its characteristics from its merchant-adventurer past, from the yeoman at the top of the family tree. It is an institution built on the trading marrow of British economic history, an institution that cultivates its acquisitions with middle-class husbandry, without fatting itself on flamboyance and eccentricity. Dr Johnson once said of Thrale's brewery (today part of the Courage group) that it was not merely 'a parcel of boilers and vats, but the potentiality of growing rich beyond the dreams of avarice'. This potentiality has certainly been fulfilled, yet the brewers have always been at pains to prove their social responsibility, their soberness in handling this wealth. Their record in public life, both nationally (at least one of the great Liberal reformers was a brewer) and locally — 'we encourage our local managers to become J.P.s or councillors' — is good. Their patronage of scientific and artistic ventures has been healthy. It was one of the Whitbreads who installed one of the very first of Boulton and Watt's 'stupendous steam engines' at their Chiswell Street brewery in London in 1775, and Whitbreads again who financed the rebuilding of the Drury Lane Theatre after it burned down in 1809.

The Beerage makes no vestigial claims to precedence; the Beerage is proud of having earned most of its rights. Its members may infuriate some city editors, one of whom has written of 'the beer barons . . . with a take-it-or-leave-it attitude', and its defence system, serried square presented to any financial marauder, may foil most outsiders' attempts to intrude. But the development of the brewing families has accurately reflected over 300 years of British social history, and the state of the industry is, in its own way, as important to, and indicative of, the British economy and way of life, as, say, the engineering or chemical industries are in theirs.

The 'mistery or art' of brewing appears to be one of those activities that have always been with us. Even Julius Caesar remarked that the Britons used vines only for arbors, and preferred to drink 'a high and mighty liquor, different from that of any other nation, made of barley and water . . . [which] leaves space enough for the performance of many great actions before the spirits are quite vanquished'. The first formal mention of the Brewers' Company appears in the City of London Letter Books of the thirteenth century. (The records of the Company contain some of the earliest known examples of written London English.) The company's first recorded tussle with authority was in 1419 with the legendary Mayor of London, Richard Whityngton, who apparently took offence at the brewers because they 'had fat swans at their feast on the morrow of St Martin, when he had none at his'. He made them sell their beer all next day at the cut-price rate of 1*d*. a gallon. 'I wish we could solve our differences with the Monopolies Commission and the Prices and Incomes Board as easily,' says one senior member of the Beerage.

Brewing has, by its nature, always been a family, if not a private affair, with publicans and innkeepers brewing their own ale. It is not, however, until the seventeenth and eighteenth centuries and the industrial revolution that the great present-day brewing families emerged from what was virtually a cottage industry. The occasional practice of some publicans of selling off excess beer to a neighbouring confrère was transformed by improving communications into a major wholesale business.

The origins of some of the great families are sometimes obscure. The first Daniel Watney, progenitor of the brewery that was the biggest in the country by the late 1950s, was said to have been abandoned as a baby by gypsies on Wimbledon Common in 1705. He was, runs the legend, discovered by a local farmer named Acres, who took him home over his saddle. The name Watney is said to be a corruption of 'What name?' Another brewer, rather smaller, in the south of England, suspects that his ancestors were horse thieves and liquor smugglers in the Scottish Highlands in the seventeenth century.

More often, however, the patriarch was a stolid 'merchant venturer bold' like John Courage who, in 1780, went to London from Aberdeen as an agent for a shipping line. Seven years later, with considerable acumen in an already overcrowded trade, he bought a small brewhouse on the south bank of the Thames, opposite the Tower of London, for £615. Or like the first Arthur Guinness, son of the agent and receiver for the Archbishop of Cashel. The archbishop left Arthur £100, which helped him to acquire the lease of a brewery in James' Gate, Dublin, 1759. The rise of the house of Guinness is quite unequalled in the Irish economy. The first Arthur's brewery had been out of action for some years when he took it over. He started with an annual production of 200 hogsheads of ale. Within five years, he had bought a country house, and was living in the style of a gentleman. After eight years, he was master of his guild.

It usually took the families only one generation or so to find themselves inextricably woven into not only the commercial life of a free trade mêlée (there were up to 300 breweries in London alone in the eighteenth century) that did not spare the lazy or the impious, but also the political history of their time. The way in which this occurred is best illustrated by the family of Samuel Whitbread (Sam One, as he is known in the family.)

Samuel came from a landed family in Bedfordshire, a county in the eighteenth century little graced with aristocracy. As one contemporary writer put it, 'If the clay, soil and clear air of Bedfordshire proved fatal to the feudal aristocracy, it continued to produce a sterner breed of famous sons, Bunyan . . . John Howard . . . Sam Whitbread.' Whitbread was, in fact, a cousin of John Howard, the penal reformer. His grandfather had fought for Cromwell, and had served as Receiver-General, and as Justice of the Peace for Bedfordshire. With £1,000, Samuel was sent to London to make his fortune. He established himself as a brewer on 11 December 1742. Eight years later, he moved to Chiswell Street, in the City, site of the present brewery.

His daughter, Mrs Gordon, wrote of him, 'In the early part of his trade, he sat up four nights in a week by his brewhouse copper, refreshed himself by washing plentifully with cold water, and a clean shirt, and when the state of the boiling permitted his quitting, retired for two hours to his closet reading the Scriptures and devotional exercises. When the rest of the world were asleep he entered the worldly business of the day, never any ways suffering the Sabbath to be broken into, either in his Counting-house, the Yard, by travelling or dissipation.' He gradually wrested from his small brewery the money to send his son Samuel (Sam Two) to Eton, and then for spells at both Oxford and Cambridge.

In 1768, Sam One was elected M.P. for Bedford, and thus began a tradition which lasted, with brief intervals, until 1910. Between those two dates, no fewer than six Whitbreads sat as M.P.s, one of them, the third Samuel, becoming Civil Lord of the Admiralty, in Lord Palmerston's last administration.

It is the second Samuel, however, who achieved lasting political fame. He entered Parliament as a radical. Mrs Betty Whitbread, wife of the present chairman, says that this situation was 'as if Anthony Eden's son had stood for Parliament as a Red'. But Samuel II's activities made him, as *The Times* remarked, 'England's greatest and most useful citizen'. His biographer, Roger Fulford, has written, 'For a decade after the death of Fox and Pitt, Whitbread dominated the House of Commons', being something of an Ombudsman, ventilator of civil rights complaints, 'leading opponent of Governmental indifference to the working classes', brother-in-law of Earl Grey, anti-war protagonist, who favoured a negotiated peace with Napoleon.

Thus, within one generation, the Whitbreads had been transformed from a parochial, if worthy, family in the Bedfordshire squirearchy, into one in the vanguard of early nineteenth-century politics. This process was the fruition of the eighteenth-century virtues, perfervid dedication to self-establishment, with a compensating piety that managed to sympathise with the working classes while mingling with the ruling class.

Col. William Whitbread, great-great-great-grandson of the founder, now chairman of Whitbreads, sees the prominence of his family in public life as a natural corollary to the county social ethos. 'Every village is made up of a school, a church and a pub, and every town is a series of villages. What happens in the pub is tremendously important, it is a great social centre. Whoever runs that pub is also extremely important to the village. The brewing families, certainly our family, came from the land. So it is quite natural that one who is producing hops and barley on the land should wish to see them made into something himself, rather than leave it to others. At the same time, the landed families were involved in local government of some sort or another for some years. I believe the activity in national public life to be an extension of this.'

The Beerage was in a unique position; while being of the trustee middle class, the natural rulers of domains not accounted for the hereditary aristocracy (although, of course, several branches of the beerage families did marry into certain titled families: indeed the second Samuel Whitbread's four daughters all married into the aristocracy) and being among the first of the modern industrial owner-entrepreneurs, they still realised that their activities, their products, their very names, affected the ordinary people at many points, at essential points. It is said that Guinness was among the camp comforts at Waterloo. Forty million cans of Courage beer were shipped to British forces in France in the 1914–18 war. The brewer's name is, quite literally, on the lips of just about every working man in this country every day of the week. The brewers may have graduated to the ruling class, but they have always been conscious that their wealth was founded on a most basic of human requirements.

No single brewing family has had quite the same fundamental attachment to the lore of a society as the Guinness family. A story is told of the dispute in early 1967 between the farmers of the west of Ireland and the Dublin Government over farm subsidy policy. The farmers formed their tractors and trailers into convoys and blocked most of the main roads. At one important road bridge, the blockade was lifted only for an ambulance, a hearse, and a lorry delivering Guinness to the local public house.

Rarely has the fortune of one family been so intertwined with the economy of its country and the lives of its populace as has that of Guinness. The setting up of the Guinness brewery was at a a time when Ireland had two economies: one of nascent industry, geared to the outside world, and the other that of rural subsistence geared to the potato. It has been said that if General Motors sneezed, America would catch a cold. It could equally facetiously be said that if a Guinness had merely sniffed during the nineteenth-century, Ireland might well have died of pneumonia. It now, it is reckoned, contributes to the livelihood of 46,700 people, although only 4,000 are directly employed. The company has not missed paying a dividend since 1759, but it has been criticised for a certain reluctance to change, to expand. One director has been heard to say, 'Why expand for expansion's sake? Size for size's sake is not a sensible thing to go after. Anyway, we're pretty big already.' Perhaps this reluctance is due to the traditional feeling that all actions, all risks undertaken by the company directly affect the economy of Ireland. In one sense, the director is quite right: the brewery is now the largest private employer in the Republic of Ireland, is the biggest exporter of beer in the world, is Ireland's biggest single exporter, and streets are named after its directors.

While the influence of Guinness on the Irish way of life (six out of every eight pints of beer consumed in the Republic are Guinness) is indeed potent, the power of the family within the firm is probably the greatest of any among the main brewing families. One writer has described the relationship between the firm and the family, as something like that between the citizens of Vienna and

Habsburg archdukes; the relationship between the brewers and the bosses like that between the Aga Khan and his racehorse trainers.

The family does retain a controlling interest in the firm, and this, in fact, is quite rare, the influence of family elsewhere being much less practical than emotional, paterfamilial, even merely nominal in some cases. The quarterly meeting of the full Guinness board has been described as 'a forest of cock's feathers and fur'.

'Oh, does that mean my aunts?' grins the Earl of Iveagh, the young chairman, sixth direct descendant of Arthur Guinness to head the company.

But this apparently unlimited power is not undiluted. There are, as Lord Iveagh points out, 30,000 stockholders in Guinness, and although the family does control, there is a large holding outside the family, indeed from outside Ireland. From the beginning, Arthur Guinness employed experts, appointed managers. From the first, he realised that because you had money, and put that money into a firm, you were not by definition best able to employ that money. So, to this day, there is a division, into an executive board and a top board. The main board, representing the major holdings, meets once every three months, while the executive board, with nine members, concerned with most decisions except those of major policy meets monthly. Lord Iveagh takes as his axiom: 'Managers should be left to manage.' Nevertheless, six of the board are members of the family, and all have a big influence. Says Lord Iveagh, 'It is not fair to say we are feudal, because it is just not true. It might be true to say we are paternalistic, although I don't like the word. But we are, in the sense of caring for the welfare of those who are working for us.'

Vast sums of money have been laid out by the Guinness

family on welfare projects for employees. (The first recorded act of philanthropy by Arthur Guinness was his advance of 250 guineas to the Dean and Chapter of St Patrick's Cathedral, Dublin, for repairs to the Chapel schools. He refused repayment, giving instead the money as premiums to the pupils of the schools.) Arthur's stout made his son, Benjamin, his country's richest man. Today, the trusts operated by the Guinness family are enormous, and include funds for large housing projects, libraries and research institutions, and restoration of cathedrals and buildings. The medieval feudal barons did often make provision for their tenants. Guinness employees are paid above the national average. A medieval serf could hardly claim that.

Sometimes, the philanthropy has been conducted in the face of efficiency. Some time ago, a management consultant recommended that the firm save itself the expense of rehousing employees sent to other localities. The company ignored this advice. The presence of family does not necessarily mean management by whim. It does, however, allow for management with consideration that other firms, with anonymous stockholders and discontinuous direction, cannot afford.

If we return to the Big Six British brewers — and Guinness is only eighth among the top brewers of the British Isles, with a total capital of just over £50 million, but, of course, Guinness only own ten public houses compared with Whitbread's 8,500 — we see that only one, Bass-Charrington, does not have a family chairman.

Whitbread is run by a seventh direct descendant of its founder. Watney-Mann chairman Peter Crossman is a descendant of Robert Crossman, who with James Mann and Thomas Paulin, formed, in the nineteenth-century, the Mann side of the enterprise. Richard Courage is a direct descendant of John Courage. Maurice Pryor, chairman of Truman, Hanbury and Buxton, is descended from Thomas and Robert Marlborough Pryor, two Quakers who joined the firm as partners in 1816. If it had not been for a superstitious sailor, the Pryors might have been obliged to set up in business abroad. For in 1660, during a time of religious persecution, Francis Pryor was taken prisoner at a meeting house and was due to be deported. The captain of the *Anne*, which was to transport him, refused to sail, however, with religious deportees aboard, fearing 'the hand of the Lord being against him'.

Sir Derek Pritchard, chairman of Allied Breweries, second biggest U.K. brewing company (an alliance of Ind Coope, Tetley and Walker and Ansells) has a family connection, albeit rather tenuous, with the firm. His own 141-year-old family wine and spirits firm, E. Halliday and Son Ltd, of Manchester, was taken over by Ind Coope in 1949 and Sir Derek has risen to the head of the alliance via the Ind Coope board.

In Alan Walker, former sugar executive, Bass-Charrington have the only 'outsider' chairman, and his experience illustrates the inherent vulnerability of the Beerage. He reports, 'In 1955, Mitchell and Butlers, who at that time were one of the most powerful provincial brewers, began to look for someone with a certain experience of commerce. Now they had seven of the family on a board of twelve. The firm was static. They were beginning to lose out to their competitors. They were terribly nice people, and I can't speak too highly of them. They thought, though, they could run a brewery, but in the context of the changing world, of course, they could not. They needed someone independent. It would be no good if you were everlastingly having to be drinking a glass of sherry or whisky with Uncle Bob or old

Charlie. I had more or less complete power. There has been, generally, a managerial change in many of those places in the nicest way, in that the families themselves divined that other people had to come in. They would eventually have been forced into it, probably by the late 1950s, but it is to their credit that they realised it before.'

With only two main exceptions, the financial control has gradually diminished. Various circumstances account for this. Death duties have often hit the brewery families very hard. Whitbreads were hit three times in two decades. By astute distribution of voting shares, however, the Whitbread family still controls the firm. Then, in some instances, members of the family itself — 'maybe an odd cousin who couldn't care less' — would cash in their shares, or the stock would pass into trusts. The interest could also be diluted by amalgamation. Before its amalgamation with Watney, the Mann group of families held about 75 per cent of the shares of their portion. The Mann-Paulin-Crossman side was about one-third of the size of the Watney branch, so the proportional interest in the firm was, overnight, cut to a fraction. The monetary interest of families in several of the major companies is now as low as 3 or 4 per cent.

There is also no doubt that whilst certain provincial brewing families still retain an iron grip of the shares and management, the families concerned with the big national groups have experienced not only dilution of financial involvement, but diminution of actual executive power. This is not to underestimate the essential function of family involvement, but it does mean an influx of outside talent to the breweries. Sons do still gravitate towards the board, but, as Alan Walker points out, in a world of changing tastes, changing commercial situations and political climate, one finds that one's own family is not necessarily best fitted to run the firm. This situation is not new to the brewers. The development of most firms, certainly during the eighteenth and nineteenth centuries, saw the rise of the brewers, the technicians, who often formed themselves into an officer class, indeed were often taken into partnership. The brewer was usually a counterbalance to the hereditary bosses. He might sometimes intimidate the owner, he might make something of an esoteric mystery of his trade, but he was an essential 'lay' influence on the great families.

This infusion of outside talent has undoubtedly had a radical effect on the Bass-Charrington group (in 1968, the biggest single brewery group in Britain, with assets of £282 million) and on the industry as a whole. Says Alan Walker, 'The main development has been a growing awareness of the need for more professionalism in management and the techniques of brewing. One of the things I found here, when I became the chairman and chief executive after it took over Mitchell and Butler, was that people still talked of being Bass men and Worthington men, even though Bass and Worthington had merged forty-two years before. They had separate notepaper, separate accounting, and separate representatives. If I have done nothing else here, I did at least knock their heads together and make them talk of the group as a whole. The main trouble — and this was the challenge, not resistance from any member of the family — was that it was very easy-going. Everything was easy-going in the 1950s, of course. Inadequate use was made of pub space. There was the tendency for the technical brewer to be kingpin. The head brewer is terribly important, but he tended to think that beer should be brewed as it has been for forty years. If a marketing man had the nerve to tell him that they could sell more if he slightly changed the colour, he would throw him out of his office. A lot of the companies have got the message that marketing is as important to the company as the actual brewing — if not more important. The advertising has greatly improved. You remember the dreary old man in the advert, with the dog in the pub and the nasty ash-tray with Woodbines painted on it? Well, that had to change.'

The main criticism shied at the beerage is that it is nepotistic. How, it is argued, can one possibly be, of necessity, gaining the best possible chairman or chief executive of your company if you are merely nominating the previous chairman's son? No qualitative evidence has ever been produced to prove that a company suffers through family succession. Indeed, the record of industrial relations in some brewing concerns would indicate just the opposite. The argument against these practices must remain emotional based on a surface view of the industry and of the families concerned. In the case of brewing, as Alan Walker says, 'Little Sam has got to be bloody good before he gets on to the board. There is probably a bit of getting Uncle So and So on to the board because he's a good scout, but much, much less now than, say, thirty years ago. In fact, there is a tendency to make it more difficult for their own progeny to become a director. After all, the company is there to make a product and to make a profit. It is not a charitable institution for the family. The competition in the industry just doesn't allow for that. It makes sense. They're not going to tolerate anyone who would jeopardise their profit, are they?'

It is worth pausing over the families' reactions to this one point, because they both illustrate the position and relevance of the hereditary beerage in Britain today, and partly answer the question of its survival in an increasingly competitive and unsentimental future.

Col. Whitbread says, 'I suppose I do feel something of a father figure here, in the sense that I have been either managing director or chairman for twenty-five years, and have therefore appointed everyone on the board. My own rule of thumb is that one is only on the board if one is good enough, no matter who he is. I was made to be a chartered accountant before I was even considered for a job here. Then I shovelled grain. My father used to say about this, 'If I have done nothing else I have stopped a lot of duds coming in.' Everyone's got to prove his own worth. My own son Michael has been a beer salesman. He will go on to the sales side, and only if he's good enough will he come on to the board. It is far more difficult for a Whitbread to get in here, they have really got to prove themselves exceptional. We are all very conscious of being from a brewing family, and we are very proud of it. I think that's why we would not let down the family tradition by appointing a dud to the board.'

Maurice Pryor, chairman of Truman's (where there are three Buxtons, three Pryors and one Hanbury on the board of nine), says, 'A member of the family only gets on to the board if he has proven specialist qualifications, and even then he must retire at sixty-five. We have an informal ten-year programme for a potential family director. He will leave his public school, then go round the world and then go to university and take degrees in science or kindred subjects, and then perhaps one in law, and then we *might* consider him. He would then be expected to work damned hard in several departments of the company. I have had one chap, one relative, asking for a job. I explained all that, and he said, 'Thank you very much' and left. It's no good running a business because you think you are entitled to do so. I knew right from the start, when I joined in the Thirties, that it was no good fooling yourself.'

Richard Courage, chairman of Courage, Barclay and Simonds (where there are two Courages and one Simonds on the parent board), says, 'I believe that the staff and employees do like to feel there is a member of the family in the chair. Someone who is personally involved in the day to day success of the firm. I do not sit on the selection panel when one of the family comes up for an appointment. But if you are involved, I think the employees feel much more secure, almost as if they feel that if the firm were to go down, then you go down too, so you fight harder for them.'

Peter Crossman, chairman of Watney, says, 'I have always accepted the fact that we should not have got very far if it had not been for family interests, but I have been clear about one thing and that is that a family director has to be that little bit better. If you get a good family director, he is unbeatable.'

Lord Iveagh says, 'My father was killed in 1945, so I succeeded my grandfather.' Lord Iveagh's grandfather, incidentally, is credited with the shortest-ever speech in the House of Lords. During a debate on country planning, one member said, 'Everywhere we go there are great signs saying, "Guinness is Good for you."' Lord Iveagh stood up and said, 'It is,' and promptly sat down. The young Lord Iveagh says, 'I was never inclined to do anything but come into the firm. I was never attracted to anything else. I was fascinated by business. Continuity is certainly one of our greatest assets. It gives a focus to the loyalty of the employees.'

A different view is taken by Sir William McEwan Younger, chairman of Scottish and Newcastle Breweries, who, although great-nephew of the founder of one of

S and N's composite firms, says, 'I do not believe in
lineal descendants automatically succeeding to a firm. I'm
a great believer in the man at the top actually running the
firm. I think the family influence creates too much danger
of the man at the top being merely nominal. It is a rela-
tively harmless system, but it is not satisfactory.'

Perhaps the most fiercely dynastic of the brewers are
the independent provincial companies. In many cases, they
have operated from those ponderous Victorian buildings,
but using ponderous Victorian management techniques,
so have disappeared. But there are still just over a hundred
small provincial breweries. Even more than in the case of
Guinness, the power of the family can be impressive.
Sometimes the board is restricted by company charter to
the family only. Sometimes the entire equity can be held
by relatives and family trusts. Two such cases are Robinsons
of Stockport and McMullens of Hertford. Their heads
are Lt-Col. Peter McMullen, a caustic, vigorous man, and
Sir John Robinson, an avuncular, yet tough-minded
north-westerner.

Peter McMullen says, 'We have just under 200 pubs
and off licences mostly in Hertfordshire. The brewery
was started in 1827 by my great-grandfather Peter. His
father was factor to the Marquess of Downshire. The
brewery has always been family controlled but our board
is not confined to family members. In 1897 it became a
public company but its ordinary shares have never been
publicly quoted on the market. There is a fearsome 'clan'
thing and if any member wishes to sell some of his shares
the Clan closes ranks and buys. When my father died just
after we returned from the War we were stung for death
duties, about half a million, and we were faced with the
decision whether to give up, and there were enormous
problems — there was no filing systems and most things

were on the back of envelopes or in my father's head — or to fight back. I think the fact that we were challenged by the death duties made us fight. We also wanted to preserve the old place of course. It took us ten years to settle and pay.

'We then had to go through a traumatic experience of pulling ourselves out of "feudalism" and to do it in the nicest possible way. At the time we were small and I knew everyone on the firm personally, but there are now about 600 employees altogether in the group and it was clear then that as we grew — as we had to — it would be impossible to run everything on entirely personal lines. Of course people can still come and kick on this door — and they often do if they want to see me personally — but we had to rid ourselves of the habit of saying that if old Joe had been in a job for twenty years, you never disturbed old Joe!

'So we all went through the whole business of job evaluation and work study and all that sort of thing and we did this many moons ago — thank goodness. We had great cooperation from all — and everyone has gained from it — but I will not disguise a feeling of intense relief that that particular period is over. Of course we still have the Work Study boys about. Our own production has increased over ten years by thirty per cent, whilst the number of our works employees has decreased by 20 per cent. But you can't run this sort of business in terms of just pounds shillings and pence. You can't because you've got local roots and because your business is "long term" and involved, through its pubs, in local communities. We sometimes make decisions which are not commercially right but we find that if they are taken for a "right" reason they usually pay off in the long run. It's not social conscience. In a way it's an investment in goodwill.

PUB

'We don't just sell drink — we sell leisure — so the pubs must be good. We decided long ago that if we were ever to go out of business we would die with good pubs. Its an expensive policy. I get around the pubs at least once a year. Some call me Mr Tea because I go at tea time when they are not busy and throw stones at their window. What I like in a pub is to be able to hear laughter and noise with doors perpetually opening and shutting. I don't like closed cliques in pubs. Also, what's wrong with the odd awkward corner? Let someone bump into someone else — maybe spill his drink. At least it gets them talking — even if only to complain about it.'

Peter McMullen is a cheerful dynast. He will walk into a pub and shout, 'Good heavens, Curly, are they still letting you in here? I thought they kicked you out years ago.' He operates from a Georgian house behind the brewery and the senior staff meet him there for a drink around seven most evenings. He believes that many an individual's problem is sorted out in a pub — by the other customers. He says, 'The pub also operates as a bank, parliament, labour exchange, welfare centre, exchange and mart, public telephone, message passer and heaven knows what else. I am sometimes surprised that they have any time left to sell beer.' He thinks that anyone in his own position needs absolute dedication, self-denial of the leisure that money can buy and 'the assessment that it is better to pass on to the children the opportunity of joining a damned good business which has cleanness and tradition than it is to give them money. Nepotism works but only if the boys are good.'

Sir John Robinson's 112-year-old Unicorn Brewery is in a narrow street near the centre of Stockport. He says, 'We are a completely family-controlled firm, and any expansion has to be financed out of our own funds. The family produces the directorate. The brewery was started by my grandfather, Frederic Robinson, just down the road from here, in the Unicorn Inn. We now have 400 pubs and off-licences. I suppose we got a start by my grandfather brewing for lazy publicans. We have grown enormously, considering our limited call on money. In 1891 we had twelve houses, in 1918 we had sixty-eight, and in the meantime, we have taken over three breweries.

'We have five directors: myself, my brother, and my three sons. We are a private company, and anyone who is not in the family cannot sit on the board. It is a matter of tradition. I was never pressurised to come into the business. I was given a completely free choice, as indeed all my sons were. This is not simple, because I was always aware — and proud — of the fact that we had territorial family associations. My first recollection was of being driven around as a small boy in a trap with my father, while he visited the managers. I would think my own boys would have the same memories. Funnily enough, I don't like beer or whisky. I am more or less teetotal. There's one thing I will not stand among my tenants, and that is drinking with the customers. We select our tenants very carefully, and I feel that they have got to set an example. I have no time for drunkenness. I come down most heavily on abuse of that description. By all means, the tenant can talk with his customer, and be friendly, but if I find a tenant habitually drinking with his customers, then he's out.

'Family succession has worked excellently. You have got to ignore the madcaps, of course, but with family succession, you are less likely to get any sort of disruption in the brewery. I think it's more satisfactory to the individual to develop himself and his ideas within a family situation than to launch himself into the unknown.

After all, what possible affinity could a young man feel with I.C.I. or a huge affair like that? Just because we have only family on the board does not mean that we have unqualified people in senior positions. All my sons are qualified in one thing or another, and our laboratories have people with magnificent qualifications. As to efficiency and so on, I must only say that we have twice compared ourselves with the big companies, and in terms of money spent on property, we are something like 2 per cent over at least one of the Big Six.'

Companies like McMullens and Robinsons seem somehow isolated from the wider financial hurly-burly. Although Peter McMullen does say, 'We have had many approaches, oh, you know, "If there's any way we can *help* you, old chap . . ." — and once, some stranger in a dark coat and astrakhan collar came here just after my father died, and came straight out with it, that he would like to buy us. I said I would arrange a meeting with my directors. I put him in a room we call the cooler, and left him there for two hours, then showed him the door.'

What annoys the brewers' critics, perhaps as much as their apparent power, is their closeness. They are all on exceptionally good terms, and share many outside interests. Col. Whitbread says, 'I remember sailing into some Scottish loch late one night, and this fellow came up alongside me. I said, "Who the hell is that?" And this voice came back, "It's Richard." It was Richard Courage.'

It is possibly this closeness, this common front, that helped the Beerage to withstand probably the biggest individual shock of its whole existence.

This 'electrifying . . . utterly shocking . . . damned impertinent . . . unbelievable' development jolted the brewers at just after six o'clock on the evening of 25 May 1959. At about that time, the then chairman of Watney,

Mr Simon Combe, received a letter from Charles Clore, which contained, in effect, a £21 million bid for Watney.

The Beerage was absolutely stunned.

Never before had its collective sway been frontally challenged. It suddenly realised that brewing was subject to precisely the same law — be it the law of the jungle — as any other industry. The property potential of the industry, the sheer mass of money that its pubs represented, came home to the Beerage in a symbolic gauntlet. The Press took the point. One commentator remarked, 'Clore . . . pin-points the dreariness of many of our . . . pubs. This is a typical sight: the bar furniture worn and shoddy. The walls smoke-stained brown, like the fingers of a forty-plus cigarettes a day man. The floor coverings threadbare and tattered. The toilets are an insult to modern hygienic society.'

The bid caught the industry completely by surprise. One Watney director was holidaying in Venice. He recalls 'I was sitting on a piazza, drinking coffee, when I caught sight of an Italian newspaper headline. I thought: It's home for me.' Maurice Pryor was motoring through the South of France, and had met up with George Mann, who was visibly shocked, he says. Richard Courage heard the news at eight o'clock that evening on the radio at home. Wherever they were, the members of the Beerage knew that an era in their life had passed. They could no longer assume that they were a caste apart, sacrosanct, able to operate on their own terms of reference and dictate.

The Watney affair developed into 'one of the fiercest battles the City has seen'. Ranks closed and the bid was withstood. Watney 'receded from his [Clore's] grasp so fast that it looks like the grin on the face of the Cheshire cat', noted the *Sunday Express*.

But not before one brewery had revalued its property,

upwards, by about 50 per cent — 'and this was conservative because we didn't want to frighten the board' —
and others by almost as much. (The bid itself had put £8
million on to Watney shares in one day.) Most of the
brewers do say that the Clore bid gave a healthy impetus
to the industry in two ways. For 300 years, it had coasted
along, carried by public taste, gradual social change, and
by its own vagaries. It was now expected to lead. Also, it
partly encouraged, partly shamed, brewers into improving their properties. Bass alone is currently spending up
to £15 million annually on property development.

The Clore bid, although a devastating — in one case,
perhaps fatal — shock to the Beerage, did not destroy it.
Centuries of accommodation, or adaptability, of entrench-
ment, of emotional pressure, would take much, much
more to undo.

But it is still a talking point in the directors' lunch
rooms, where conversation so much resembles that of
both Oxford High Table and the officers' wardroom. The
portraits gradually increase, and, through each season,
the grouse gradually decrease. The spectre of financial
Visigoths displacing the nebulous autocracy is exorcised.

The imperatorial cloak still rests easily on the shoulders
of the Beerage.

⚙⚙

'Damn Rommel, where's the beer?'

COL. GRAFTEY-SMITH
Commanding 3rd County of London Yeomanry
Before Alamein